# MANAGING
# BY
# INFLUENCE

## Kenneth Schatz
## and
## Linda Schatz

Prentice-Hall, Inc.          Englewood Cliffs, New Jersey

Prentice-Hall International, Inc., *London*
Prentice-Hall of Australia, Pty. Ltd., *Sydney*
Prentice-Hall Canada, Inc., *Toronto*
Prentice-Hall of India Private Ltd., *New Delhi*
Prentice-Hall of Japan, Inc., *Tokyo*
Prentice-Hall of Southeast Asia Pte. Ltd., *Singapore*
Whitehall Books, Ltd., Wellington, *New Zealand*
Editora Prentice-Hall do Brasil Ltda., *Rio de Janeiro*
Prentice-Hall Hispanoamericana, S.A., *Mexico*

© 1986 *by*

Purpose, Inc.

**Library of Congress Cataloging-in-Publication Data**

Schatz, Kenneth.
  Managing by influence.

  Includes index.
  1. Psychology, Industrial.   2. Influence (Psychology)
3. Management.   4. Supervision of employees.
I.  Schatz, Linda.   II. Title.
HF5548.8.S34   1986      658.4'09        86-12199

ISBN   0-13-550591-7

Printed in the United States of America

*In Loving Memory Of*
JOSHUA G. SCHATZ
*February 26, 1910 – January 15, 1983*

*A Messenger for the Community*

# Acknowledgments

We are deeply grateful to the Schatz and Company Board of Overseers for their unending support, feedback, advice, and encouragement in everything we do. Dear friends and sound business counselors, they were enthusiastic throughout the entire writing project and never lost faith. They are: Mort Ehudin, Bob Hughes, Pat Kogod Hughes, Beverly Nerenberg, Jacques Rebibo, Skip Schatz, and Stanley Snyder.

Our outstanding agent, Michael Snell, stayed with us while mixing inspiration with cold facts in just the right ratio. He is an excellent teacher and a master at taking care of worried authors.

We greatly appreciate the assistance of Barry Scher at Giant Food. Many thanks also are due to everyone at Giant and The Rouse Company who contributed to this book.

In the early stages, Patricia Aburdene, Gray Jacobik, and Bruce Gregory provided heart-lifting inspiration and valuable guidance. The Washington Independent Writers organization introduced us to the world of publishing with their important information and suggestions.

At Prentice-Hall, our editor, Tom Power, had the vision to understand our work and help us prepare it for the marketplace. And Kathy Dix, the production editor, greatly improved the manuscript with her detailed corrections.

Finally, our clients have our enduring gratitude. They've all been successful in the Managing By Influence™ programs, achieving significant results for themselves while giving us the satisfaction of being their partners along the way. Each of our client companies is dear to us. We've all learned together. Thanks.

# How to Be More Effective Managing By Influence

Sidney Rittenberg spent sixteen years in prison in China, fifteen of them in solitary confinement. When he returned to the United States after being freed, people asked him how he kept his sanity during all those years of solitary. Rittenberg responded that each day he tried to set some time aside to think quietly about life.[1]

Imagine a man in solitary confinement needing to set time aside to reflect on life. If he needed it, what about you? What time have you set aside to think quietly about your life as a leader?

Not many managers follow Mr. Rittenberg's policy. We offer this book as an opportunity to inventory your leadership and to rediscover your innate power to be successful as a manager. You will gain more control of your organization— whether it's one department or the whole company.

This book enables you to more skillfully manage your organization, applying your influence to create a climate of company commitment and openness to change. You'll see how to involve your management and staff, easing the burden felt when your responsibility seems greater than your control. Ultimately, you'll stay out of the details by effectively managing the climate. You'll lead your organization to make important change, quickly. You'll use your influence to reduce employee cynicism and a "protect-your-turf" attitude. You'll also improve your management of conflict resolution and problem solution.

Our clients, using the same techniques and recommendations presented in this book, have achieved results ranging from outstanding to miraculous. While participating in our Managing By Influence™ seminars and programs, they've accomplished these remarkable results not from complicated, complex formulae and equations of management, but by applying our lessons and tools directly and honestly.

After gaining new knowledge about their leadership, these managers have attained broad benefits. You'll do the same, gaining such benefits as:

  –Developing open, direct communication

  –Getting problems solved at lower levels

  –Increasing initiative from below

  –Encouraging people to make bolder use of their authority

  –Reducing friction between departments

  –Working toward common goals

  –Renewing the challenge of the job

Ultimately, these benefits mean improved productivity, quality, revenues, and profit.

Leadership is the total effect you have on the people and events around you. This effect is your influence. Effective leading is being consciously responsible for your organizational influence. Most managers don't realize how much influence they have. They feel their organizations are slipping out of their control. Through a combination of techniques, self-evaluations, and action steps, our book will show you how to achieve far more influence and leadership than you've ever experienced in the past.

Chapter 1 helps you overcome the gap managers feel between their authority and their influence. You will assess your own influence and attitudes until you can lead your organization with more potency.

Chapter 2 reveals The Question of Influence—a technique to find and develop new links between you and your organization. You'll gain more control in your job. Actually, you will be *regaining* control. And you'll see proof that you were born with enough leadership—it's just a question of using it effectively.

In Chapter 3, you'll learn the techniques of the first Managing By Influence lever, Leading to Change. This means lasting change, not cosmetic change. You'll learn the tools and concepts needed to lead others to step out of character for the good of the organization and create a new beginning. You'll be able to break the inertia of the past which often keeps things going "the way we've always done them."

The second lever, Managing the Climate, is developed in Chapter 4. You'll learn a technique called "Climate Check" which enables you to monitor the environment of the workplace and have leverage over moment-to-moment affairs through the art of small, masterful actions. Chapter 5 contains twelve strategies for creating the climate which you can select, adapt, and use in your own organization.

Chapter 6 reveals the third lever, Promoting Commitment, the most subtle and powerful leadership instrument. You'll enhance your ability to evoke the natural commitment people already have to their workplace. After reading the ten strategies and some do's and don'ts of promoting commitment in Chapter 7, you will be able to lead your organization to more committed behavior, using the finesse of leverage.

Our lessons are like getting a good joke—once you realize its import, it's yours. This is a relatively simple book, but it is not a humble one. In reading it, you will gain tools for major, unalterable steps ahead in your ability to lead. It doesn't matter where you are in your ability to lead—very advanced or way back in the pack. Regardless of where you are, there's improvement to be made.

We'll present you with techniques to appraise yourself and your present attitudes. You'll see where you've limited yourself and how to make adjustments. Without a foundation of self-recognition and an understanding of basic concepts, techniques have no value. This book provides that foundation and supplies the tools necessary for applying the leadership techniques of MBI to your organization.

## Tips for Success

The secret to successful use of this book is observing yourself as objectively as possible, even using others to help you see yourself. You will never know if this book works for you until you've actually used the tools and techniques of MBI. The trick will be to have the persistence to try out what you learn long enough for it to become second nature to you. According to Maxwell Maltz in *Psycho-Cybernetics,* this takes twenty-one days.[2] You may forget many of the specifics, but the experience that becomes second nature to you will be valuable forever. Therefore, test your MBI skills for at least three weeks before you make your final judgement on how well our techniques are working for you. To assist you in monitoring your progress, we've included a self-appraisal in Appendix 1.

We subscribe to the philosophy that you're either moving ahead in life or you're falling behind. Some leaders lull themselves into complacency, trying to hang onto the status quo. Satisfied with things as they are, these people lose the drive that brought them success. We believe this is a mistake. When you commit yourself to the status quo, you're destined to lose ground. So there are only two possibilities: moving ahead or falling behind. This book is a vehicle that will keep you moving ahead.

We know that if you approach the book with a determination to make it valuable in your own life, you too will achieve noteworthy benefits and a renewed challenge and sense of satisfaction from work well done. We'd be delighted to hear from you.

Ken and Linda Schatz
Schatz and Company
Alexandria, VA

# Contents

# 1

# Understanding the Gap Between Authority and Influence

In 1959, the Green Bay Packers hired a new head coach. Vince Lombardi took virtually the same team that had won only one game in 1958 to a 7-5 season in 1959, then to the national championship game in 1960

In managing the Packers, Coach Lombardi had no more authority than the previous coach. Both had the right to tell the players and assistant coaches what to do and how to do it. But Lombardi's use of his *influence* led the team to new commitment, uncharacteristic behavior, and victory. From 1961 to 1969, Lombardi built a legend from the nucleus of a team that couldn't win before he took the helm.

Managers can accomplish results in one of two ways: through authority—the right or power to command thought, opinion, or behavior; or through influence—the power to produce results *without* the direct use of force or command.

Most managers trust their influence less than their authority. Even though they know they have the right to tell people how to behave on the job, they often lack the ability to elicit that behavior, and, as a result, feel they have too little real influence and control.

Managing by authority implies direct controlling and

1

maneuvering toward a desired result. Managing by influence, on the other hand, means the ability to produce results by indirect or intangible means—to sway. While Vince Lombardi's management style employed force and authority, his most important work was accomplished through influence. He was a master at coaching by influence.

---

The leadership style of Giant Food's Chief Executive Officer, Israel Cohen, differs radically from that of Vince Lombardi. Izzy—as he's known to all of the 20,000 employees—presides over the chain's 144 supermarkets like a benevolent, favorite uncle. Yet through his influence, Giant has become the industry trendsetter. National companies have been forced out of Giant's Washington-Baltimore area market, and the main competitor, Safeway, has raised its level of service in an attempt to catch up.

Giant is no slouch at making a profit, either. Average after-tax profit in the supermarket industry is 1 percent; Giant consistently doubles this to 2 percent. Israel Cohen has led his team to victory through a family-oriented management style, and through influence.

---

If you live in a big or moderately big city, you've probably benefitted from something built by The Rouse Company, a leader in real estate development. Shopping centers and urban "happenings" such as Harborplace in Baltimore, Faneuil Hall in Boston, and South Street Seaport in New York get rave reviews from locals and tourists alike. Each of these projects has had a major impact on the city as well as the shopping community. Rouse has built other noteworthy regional shopping malls in cities such as Milwaukee, St. Louis, and Santa Monica and developed the "new town" of Columbia, Maryland, now a city of 64,000.

Rouse combines two aspects that few other developers are able to achieve concurrently. The Rouse Company projects manifest the vision to be new, exciting, and of very high quality. But they also emphasize the bottom line: financial success for both owners and tenants.

Bruce Alexander, senior vice-president, manages the Commercial Development Division which produces these projects. His style is very professional, direct, and even. The division uses matrix management which, by its nature, blurs authority lines. And Alexander's people work around the entire country, so he does not have much time to spend directly on each project. The success of his management depends on his use of influence to provide the drive for commitment, extraordinary teamwork, and accomplishment.

## SIX STEPS TO EXPANDING YOUR INFLUENCE

Leadership is the total effect you have on the people and events around you. This effect is your influence. Effective leading is being consciously responsible for your organizational influence. The steps to expanding your influence involve an understanding of the separation between authority and influence, followed by an examination of your present leadership impact.

### Step 1: Compare Your Influence to Your Authority

To have the ability to manage by influence, you must distinguish between the effect of your authority and the effect of your influence. When you find that your influence is less than your authority and responsibility, you're in trouble. Your organization has escaped from your control.

This may explain the Peter Principle, which says you rise to your level of incompetence. Because most managers advance on the basis of their personal strength and technical abilities, they can manage a small group by hands-on management, and still remain technically strong. Their personal supervision is enough to keep the group under control. As they succeed and get promoted, they reach a point where they can't personally oversee all the work of the larger group.

Now they need to rely on management skills. Yet, in many cases, these business strengths have not been fully developed and there's no time to stop and build them. So these managers forge ahead—with their organizations slightly out of control.

These executives have authority and responsibility, but not enough influence. Often, they just try to exert more authority. If you've done this, you know it simply doesn't work beyond a certain point. You become a juggler, throwing more balls into the air moment by moment. But the time soon comes when you just can't handle any more. Then it's time to begin managing by influence.

*Self-Check*

*Is your influence as great as your authority and responsibility? To find out, ask yourself these questions:*

> *—Do I ever feel things are out of my control?*
>
> *—Do I ever think: If I had my way, things would be different around here?*
>
> *—Do I ever feel I just can't get people to do things the way I'd like them to be done?*

After all, since you have the authority, everything must be going the way you want. Right? Probably not. Most managers say, "It's not all going my way." So you see the gap between your *right to command* behavior and your *ability to evoke* behavior.

---

## MBI ACTIONS

**#1.** List three specific incidents where you had the authority to give someone an assignment but, even as you assigned it, felt you didn't have the influence to get it done your way.

## Step 2: Use Influence Without Authority

Let's take a closer look at authority and influence to find out what really gets the job done. Managers are often uncertain about how they get results. Having authority clouds the issue, yet some might think that enough authority can get the job done regardless of influence.

Consider the salesperson. He or she produces results without any authority. After all, how much authority does the salesman have over his prospect? None—no right or power to command behavior. If he did have authority, he would just call prospects and command, "Order 30 units of our Model 136-JS!"

So the salesman walks into a prospect's office armed with nothing more than influence. How much influence does a salesman have over the prospect? A lot. In fact, if he's a *good* salesman, he assumes he has 100 percent influence. What would you call him if he assumed he had no influence? A clerk—a cashier.

A good salesman assumes he has 100 percent influence as he meets with a prospect. But suppose he doesn't make the sale. How much influence did he have? You might say "none" or "not enough." When he goes into the next prospect's office, how much influence does a *good* salesman assume he has? Again, 100 percent! Why? Because, since he has no authority, he's forced to rely once more on his influence. It wouldn't make any sense for him to assume he has no influence. If he did that, he might as well stay home. (And that's exactly what bad salespeople do!)

Managers, on the other hand, do have authority and often attempt to manage using only their authority. In fact, some managers act as if they have no influence, just authority. They go out and wield only their authority. And if a little doesn't work, they try wielding more.

### *Self-Check*

*Do you sometimes act as if you had no influence, only authority? Ask yourself:*

   *—Do I ever wonder why an employee
   hasn't done what I asked? I've already
   told the employee three times to do it!*

   *—If I get the sense that one of my people
   will not carry out an assignment the
   way I want it done, do I ever just talk
   more loudly and firmly?*

   *—Do I ever give assignments and then just
   let the chips fall where they may, while I
   sit back and hope for the best?*

When you think you need to fall back on your authority to accomplish something, remember: the salesperson performs his or her entire task using influence alone.

---

### MBI ACTIONS

**#2.** Review each of the three incidents you just listed. What might you have done differently if you had assumed you had 100 percent influence?

---

### Step 3: Recognize That Your Influence Can Undermine Your Authority

A Boston dentist, whom we'll call Dave Levine, was frustrated because his staff kept coming in late. He gathered his seven people and said, "From now on, there's a new rule around here. Everyone must be at work by 8:15. Is that clear?" His staff told him they understood. The next morning, however, Levine didn't bother to check if anyone was late. The following day he saw someone come in late but he didn't confront her. This continued for several days.

He had said by his authority that everyone must be in by 8:15, but his actions told a different story. The staff kept coming in late. What really affected the staff: Levine's authority or his influence?

Suppose he never told anyone to come in on time, but kept a close eye on people coming in and always brought it to their attention when they arrived after 8:15. Suppose he thanked people for being in before 8:15. Wouldn't this say something without Levine's ever "using his authority" to make the rule? It isn't very efficient, but it would get the job done. The truth is, influence always leads to results.

———

A company, call it Shoe World of Houston, hired a new manager for one store—thereby giving him authority to manage the store. Marianne Williams, the firm's president, found that every time the new manager, Ed, had a problem, he would call her. She would solve the problem, and he would carry out her solution perfectly. The only catch: he wasn't solving problems without her.

Soon, Williams realized she had an extra drain on her— Ed and his problems. She started to think she had made a mistake in hiring Ed, and considered replacing him. If he couldn't do the job she had given him, he was no help to her. She was going to tell him about her unhappiness, but after some thought, decided to try a different tactic.

On Ed's next call about a problem, Williams asked how *he* would solve it. He devised an answer that she thought would work, and she told him to go ahead with it. Williams was delighted. The next time he called, she did the same thing, and it worked again. After two more weeks of this, Ed stopped calling on her to solve problems.

Williams gained respect for Ed, and several months later she asked him why he was calling her so much at first. He told her, "On my first day, you told me, 'Anytime you have a problem, call me.' I did, and you seemed very happy to solve the problem. I called again and you acted pleased about being directly involved, so I kept on working with you that way. I thought that's what you wanted. I was going to suggest that I make more decisions, but I wanted to wait a few months till I felt more secure. Then you started to trust me, and I didn't need to mention it to you."

Marianne Williams saw how careful she had to be about little things she said that could influence people and cause trouble. She began considering the possibility that everything she does has an impact. She started finding little things to do to cause success.

---
### MBI ACTIONS

**#3.** Review your three incidents to recognize what previous action of yours might have undermined your authority. (For example, you may not have confronted the person the last time an assignment was mishandled.)

---

### Step 4: Enhance the Influence You Already Have

Scientists say you use 20 percent or less of your brain. To be smarter, you don't need a brain transplant. You just need to use more of what you have. There are proven exercises that can help you use your brain more.

Physicians say you use 20 percent or less of your lung capacity. To be healthier, you don't need a lung transplant. You just need to exercise more—like aerobics or yoga breathing—so you can use more of the lungs you already have.

We say that you use 20 percent or less of your influence. To be a stronger, more effective leader—to exert more influence—you don't need an "influence transplant." You don't need to become Abe Lincoln. You just need to learn how to use more of what you already have. You need to use more of your born leadership.

At first, realizing that you use so little of your influence may sound like bad news, but there's good news in it also. If you can increase the use of your influence from the present 20 percent up to 22 percent, that's an increase of 2/20ths or 10 percent. Wouldn't it be wonderful to increase your effectiveness by 10 percent? Especially if you're already doing a good job.

Ten percent more influence would make a big difference for most managers. It would provide an opportunity to achieve results that they've given up on as impossible.

## Step 5: Identify Leadership Opportunities

What are the implications of greater influence on your part? Let's consider this by discussing different approaches to opening a locked door. If a door were locked and you were told to open it, but you had no key, how would you do it?

You might use a cannon and blow it open. If you did, you'd be able to say, "I got the job done!" But there are some undesirable side effects: ruined door, damaged ceiling, no more door jamb, lots of cleanup.

If, however, you had the key, would you choose the cannon? Of course not! You only use harsh means when a lighter, gentler way isn't available.

The same holds true for your leadership and influence. Sometimes you're faced with job situations that seem to require a cannon because you haven't found the key. But knowing the cost of the cannon—employee turmoil and distrust, permanent scars and broken relationships, possibly the resignation of an employee—you leave the door closed and proceed, even though slightly handicapped by the loss of the room beyond the door. You're satisfied that the cost of the harsh, authoritative action would be greater than the gain.

As you reclaim more of your influence, you'll discover more keys. You'll be able to gently open doors that you felt were closed forever. The key is influence.

---
### MBI ACTIONS
---

**#4.** List three issues in your organization that you've given up on because you don't know how to improve them without the probability of doing too much other damage.

---

## Step 6: Confront Your Influence

When you use 20 percent of your brain and lungs, the 80 percent you are not using doesn't affect you. Influence is different. You use 20 percent of your influence *consciously*. But with influence, the 80 percent you don't consciously use *does* affect your work. The 80 percent you are not consciously using, you are *unconsciously* using!

When you are the boss, you are *never* without influence:

## YOU CAN NEVER NOT LEAD

Everything you do, and everything you *don't* do, has an effect. You lead by acts of *commission,* and you lead by acts of *omission.* You are always leading and influencing.

In fact, your best acts of commission may be completely undone by your acts of omission. Go back to Dave Levine, DDS, and his employee-lateness problem. His influence actually undermined what he was trying to accomplish with his authority. By not checking for lateness or confronting it, his acts of omission said that his act of commission was void. His *unconscious* influence took a heavy toll.

———

Leadership is the total effect you have on the people and events around you, regardless of your authority. In this light, leadership is influence. It differs radically from hands-on management or direct supervision.

You influence all of your people all the time. But this should come as no great surprise. Great teachers and thinkers have always told us that our every action affects the world around us. Managers need to be particularly aware of this fact. Indeed, many things may occur at your company that you would like to think happen *in spite* of you, not *because* of you.

So, even though you have 100 percent authority, not everything happens the way you want it to. Does this mean there is a gap between your authority and your influence? No and yes. No: you have 100 percent influence, and you can never not lead, so a gap never appears. Yes: you use only 20 percent of your influence consciously, so a gap does separate your authority and the amount of conscious influence you are exerting.

The sum of your influence—conscious and unconscious—totals 100 percent. It is so pervasive that you seldom stop to take account of it. Perhaps you've been so busy seeing what you think are signs of your lack of influence that you've lost sight of the proof of your influence. To gain a new objectivity, it's time to think quietly about your life as a leader.

You gain extraordinary power when you take conscious responsibility for the fact that you are always Managing By Influence.

*Self-Check*

*Take a moment to look at your own situation. Ask yourself:*

> —*After I've delegated authority, do I often feel that I've lost control over the work?*
>
> —*While I understand in principle that the small things I do may have a big effect, am I uncertain how this works in specific cases?*
>
> —*If a situation can't be resolved without heavy use of authority, do I ever just let it go and tolerate it?*

## WHY YOU ALWAYS USE YOUR INFLUENCE

Picture this. A mother is standing on the curb with her two-year-old. The child steps into the street and the mother says, "No, no," bringing the child back to the curb. A moment later the youngster steps into the street again, and once again the mother says, "No, no," and returns the child to safety.

This happens five more times and the mother tires of telling the child "No," so she looks the other way for a moment. The child steps into the street while the mother is looking the other way. The child decides, "It's okay for me to go into the street once in a while, especially if I wear Mommy out first."

That's not the message Mommy wanted to give! She just wanted to give them both a break. After all, she didn't *tell* the child to walk into the street. But the one time she didn't tell the two-year-old *not* to walk into the street, the child still read meaning into it.

Too bad. When you're a mother, you can never not lead. Parents influence their children all the time. That's the bad news and the good news, just as it is with all leaders.

---

## MBI ACTIONS

**#5.** Recognizing that you can never not lead, review the items you've listed. Make a plan to rectify items in progress by taking influential actions. If you're not sure how, set the list aside until you've read further.

---

### RECOGNIZING WHEN YOU'RE IN CONTROL

People usually perceive Harry Truman's famous quote, "The buck stops here," as more of a burden than a blessing. You can think of it as bad news: "No matter what happens, I get the final responsibility, even if it was out of my control." In reality, that "bad news" can lead to "good news."

You really are 100 percent influential and responsible— in control. You can never not lead, and therefore, the buck does stop with you. Settle on the full meaning of *The buck stops here,* and you win a prize. Good news: The buck not only stops here, the buck *starts* here, too. You can make it come out any way you want for the good of your organization—you are in control!

### HOW TO USE LEVERAGE WHEN MANAGING BY INFLUENCE

A lever is a tool, like a bottle cap opener, that helps you apply your strength to big jobs that you couldn't do otherwise. Typically, you push on the long end to move something on the short end, as with first gear in a car. It gives you the ability to start your car moving and to drive up steep hills. When you use a lever, you gain the ability to move a heavy load.

Managing by authority, with hands-on and direct supervision, provides this type of leverage. But you have to move your end a long way to achieve a small movement at the other end. You wouldn't want to drive from San Francisco to Los Angeles in first gear. Using a lever this way can tie you up.

Managing By Influence employs a more powerful type of leverage. When you discover your full influence, you find out how to accomplish big results through *little* movements on your part, recognizing a power you didn't realize you had. You learn how the little things you do, or don't do, create big results, freeing you to get more done in less time. Grab the short end of the stick and you'll get a lot of work done.

Managing By Influence incorporates three specific levers.

### Lever 1: Leading to Change

According to a Chinese proverb, "If we keep going the way we're going, we're likely to wind up where we're headed." Unfortunately, most companies keep going the way they *were* going even when they want to head someplace new. Not only has the past brought them the present, it's also leading them to the future. They continue on the same path because they've "always done it that way."

Vince Lombardi found a way to lead the Packers out of their losing attitude. As individuals and as a team, they were able to step out of character. He evoked a team effort from free spirits like running back Paul Hornung and receiver Max McGee. He had the ability to break with the past in his own mind, and to lead others to a new future. Says linebacker Ray Nitschke, "He helped turn me around as a person."[1]

Chapter 3 presents The Change Triangle, which helps managers lead people to be open to change. You'll learn three critical techniques to carry yourself and others from old notions about the past to a new ability to step out of character—to go beyond old limits. The Change Triangle focuses on people's power to excel when they act for a purpose larger than their own needs—as in a team sport or as our U.S. athletes did in the 1984 Olympics. In business, this means acting for the good of the company.

You'll find these techniques useful in leading your people and in adjusting your own attitudes. The Change Triangle begins with the fact that you're always leading, so you can first examine how you've contributed to the present openness to change—or the lack of it.

### Lever 2: Managing the Climate

Suppose you had the job of wetting the leaves of 1,000 house plants. You could take some pails of water and sponges and get to work. Or, you might get more sophisticated and use a hose. Still, it would take a lot of work.

Now, consider this approach: Raise the relative humidity of the room to 100 percent and then drop the temperature ten degrees. In that climate, everything gets wet! If you generate the right environment, things naturally fall into place. If you get it wrong, things naturally don't work out. A cactus won't do well in the climate you just produced.

By creating the appropriate environment, you've used leverage over many details. With this type of influence, managers can take little actions to affect the environment, to bring about big results. But first you must accept responsibility for the existing condition, remembering that YOU CAN NEVER NOT LEAD. Chapter 4 discusses how you influence your people through the climate of your organization. You'll learn about Climate Check, a technique for monitoring the environment. In Chapter 5, you'll get twelve strategies for creating your climate and tips on how to implement them. Managing the climate makes maximum use of your leverage.

Giant Food CEO Izzy Cohen can't be at every store everyday. So Giant devised a campaign called "Company's Coming" by which Cohen and top management visit each of the 144 stores once a year. The goals are to show the people that management cares and to create a climate of perfection and service. Says Cohen, "After all, I don't serve any customers—

our employees really do all the work. The least I can do is be involved with them."

## Lever 3: Promoting Commitment

The final lever of influence proves to be the most potent, the most subtle, and the most difficult one to master. Promoting commitment enables managers to lead people to work together with common interest. It also evokes a sense of involvement and ownership that creates fulfillment for everyone in the organization.

No one is 100 percent committed to the company. Not even the boss. But everyone does have some commitment. So where should managers focus: on the part that's committed or on the part that's not committed? By focusing on the employees' existing commitment, you can bring out more commitment in your organization. Many leaders spotlight the part of people that's not committed. Treat people as if they're not committed, and lo and behold, they're not. After all, as boss, you lead the way.

Dr. Dave Levine eventually resolved the lateness problem by recognizing that his staff was as committed to the success of the practice as he was. In the past, he had always assumed that he was the only one who really cared. When he focused on the staff's commitment to the practice, he merely sat down with them and asked how they felt about lateness. They worked it out as if they, too, owned the practice. What a burden off Levine!

At The Rouse Company, Bruce Alexander promotes common commitment to make matrix management work. Every project uses staff managers from several different departments. And most of these managers work on several projects at the same time. As a result, many people work for more than one development director in addition to a department manager. Each person reports to a minimum of two bosses.

This system permits flexibility and puts outstanding talent onto each project, making optimum use of division expertise. It can also cause confusion. After all, each person can have a split loyalty to several projects and to his own department. But, since the proof of the pudding is in the eating, one look at a Rouse project shows that Alexander is good at managing the division with the matrix system.

What happens when the needs of several projects conflict? How do you allocate resources if you're Bruce Alexander? More important, how do you create a situation where the department managers and development directors resolve these matters without you?

Alexander does it by promoting commitment to the division. Naturally, the division is only one part of The Rouse Company and must fit into the company's goals, but within the division he leads people to the understanding that they are each responsible for the success of the entire division.

He makes sure that his managers are willing to put all their behavior to the test: what's in the best interest of the division? Alexander knows that they all have a commitment to their projects, to their departments, to the company, and to their own personal needs and egos. But, he also knows that they have a commitment to the Commercial Development Division. He can focus on whichever commitment he wants to, and he recognizes that the only useful focus for the boss is the common commitment—the division.

When he does this, everyone can find a common ground without needing Alexander's involvement in minor differences and potential standoffs between peers. All he needs to do is keep people focused on what they have in common. That's good leverage for Bruce Alexander. While he'll never have enough time to work out every detail, he does have the time to promote common commitment.

Chapter 6 probes the issue of commitment and develops a deep understanding of its benefit to any organization. Commitment leads to communication, problem solution and conflict resolution. It also cures cynicism. Chapter 7 teaches ten strategies and techniques for managers to promote commitment.

## RECOGNIZING YOUR PRESENT INFLUENCE

Since you can never not lead, you're already using Managing By Influence leverage—perhaps *unconsciously*. The many small things you do and don't do each day affect your organization—affect its openness to change, its climate, and its expression of commitment.

Before you begin to learn and use these "new" techniques, it's important to recognize how you're *already* using these levers of influence—even without realizing it.

## HOW LITTLE ACTIONS CAN HELP YOUR LEADERSHIP

A small Midwestern college got a new president three years ago, call him Alan Hundert. The beauty of the campus delighted him, but he was also struck by a lot of unsightly litter.

Without raising the issue to anyone—students, faculty, or maintenance crew—Hundert began picking up any litter he saw. As he drove up the long entrance road, he'd stop his car and get out to pick up trash. Whenever he walked anywhere on campus, he'd stop, bend over, and pick up litter. He'd go off the walkways and pick up debris.

The first response came from the maintenance crew. Very soon the driveway was free of litter without his efforts. Over the first year, Hundert noticed that he was no longer bending over to pick up trash. The campus was clean. People had stopped littering. And he had never used his authority as president to make a rule, put up signs, or delegate the problem to someone else.

Hundert was so excited about his success that he decided to start a new personal campaign his second year. He made it the year of smiling and saying hello. He had noticed that students, faculty, and staff tended to look grim and unfriendly. He also recognized that since he had arrived, Hundert had fit himself into this existing culture. It no longer suited him. Alan Hundert set out to promote a climate of friendliness at the college.

He always considered it to be an important part of his job to get around the school and not stay holed up in his office. So it was easy to just add his new touch when he went out. He said hello to everyone, smiled, and, when possible, shook hands. It took several months before he noticed any difference, but then he saw that the people who were nearest him had begun acting friendlier to one another. More months went by and he watched and kept it up. He also started telling people that the college was a friendly place. By the end of the year, it was.

Not only did Hundert get his results, he achieved much more. He recognized that he could get his job done through subtle means. This is particularly important at a college, because the lines of authority are historically fuzzy, and authority tends to be resented by both students and faculty. Alan Hundert now sees that he can get his job done, managing by influence.

## UNDERSTANDING THE ESSENCE OF LEADERSHIP

The essence of leadership is knowing that YOU CAN NEVER NOT LEAD. You have 100 percent influence, all of the time. You lead by acts of commission and by acts of omission.

All other information about leading takes second place to this. Until you understand this, and understand your responsibility for things as they are now and as they have been, you'll never lead with your full potential. You can't get new control of your organization until you recognize that it's always been in your control, even if you were not aware of it. As we explain how to manage by influence, we'll go into some details and techniques, but it will always come back to this. If you learn nothing more than this, and come to grips with it more deeply than you ever have before, you will become a more effective manager.

Chapter 2 will introduce The Question of Influence to

enable you to discover how you affect, moment to moment, the organization you manage. The remaining chapters will develop the three Managing By Influence levers.

---

─────────── **MBI ACTIONS** ───────────

**#6.** Think of a time when you did something that seemed very small and unimportant to you but later had significant results. It might have been a "thank you" that changed someone's attitude. Or you may have included someone in a meeting to which he or she normally wouldn't have been invited, and it turned that person on to a level of involvement you didn't expect. Use the lessons of this chapter to plan and take a small action which will produce big results. Prove to yourself that you can never not lead.

**#7.** Now, look for a time when you took no action, and your lack of action produced a positive or negative outcome that you hadn't expected. It may have been a matter of very little consequence to you at the time, something you did quite unconsciously, that meant a lot to others. How could you have been more conscious of the impact your lack of action would have?

Purposely take "no action" to influence one of your people.

# 2

# How to Use Your Influence to Increase Your Impact

Vince Lombardi said, "Contrary to the opinion of many people, leaders are not born. Leaders are made, and they are made by effort and hard work."[1] What type of effort and hard work does it take to make you into a better leader? It takes an objective look at yourself, perhaps the hardest work there is in life, but also the most fruitful for growth. Then it takes the effort to apply appropriate techniques and practice.

You need courage to look at yourself objectively, to see how well you're accomplishing your mission. In the case of your leadership, it means taking responsibility for everything that happens in your organization.

As you find the links between yourself and your organization and discover more influence than you thought you had, you can adjust your attitudes and behavior. While these changes may require effort, most people find that the difficult part is in the discovery.

## HOW ONE MANAGER USED INFLUENCE TO SOLVE A SERVICE PROBLEM

A senior manager of a national supermarket chain, call it Quality Markets, realized that customer service had declined on Sundays. Beverly Patley was vice-president of New York operations. Patley knew it wasn't that store managers didn't care, but Sunday was a double-time day which caused budgets to run tight. Besides, every manager knew that "customers don't expect as much service on Sundays." Well, this wasn't what Patley and Quality Markets stood for.

Patley decided to act. She put herself on duty every fourth Sunday and began touring stores. Very shortly, zone directors started the same routine every fourth Sunday. Patley knew she didn't have to do it, but it said to her people that if it's important enough for me to get out, it's important to you, Mr. or Ms. Store Manager, to make sure your store is running right. You don't have to work every Sunday, but it's a good idea to stop by your store, just to satisfy yourself. This is your store. If you owned the business, you would go in. You would make sure everything was properly taken care of. That's how we want you to treat it—as though it's your business.

In several weeks, Beverly Patley was satisfied that the service had turned around. Rather than start a survey, investigation, or campaign pointed at others, Patley simply asked herself what she was doing or not doing to cause a lower level of customer service, and then how she could change herself to make it better.

Patley acted as if what she did made a difference and used the leverage of influence to affect her many stores. By questioning her own part in the undesired situation, she brought it under control.

## LAYING THE GROUNDWORK FOR EXPANDING YOUR INFLUENCE

Athletic training teaches an important lesson in how to expand your abilities. A major advance in training has come from the use of video and film replays.

When a long-distance runner discovers by replay that she is swinging her feet unnecessarily to the right and left, she makes a conscious plan to correct it. The secret to greater endurance is revealed. But, even without thinking about it, she also unconsciously begins work on correcting it.

When a boxer sees that he's lowering his left arm before throwing a right, thereby telegraphing the punch and dropping his guard, he trains to change that. The solution to the problem has been found. But, in addition to these obvious efforts, he makes less obvious, unconscious adjustments just from having made the discovery.

When you discover how your acts of commission or omission caused one of your people to fail at the job you assigned him or her, you consciously begin to alter your own behavior. The cure for the failure has been found. And just like other people, you also make unconscious adjustments.

The expansion of your abilities through a combination of conscious and unconscious corrections begins with an objective study of yourself in action, comparing your conscious use of influence to your 100 percent total influence. You then begin work on the part you employ unconsciously. Since you're already successful, you must be naturally good at leading—even unconsciously. If you weren't, you'd be long gone.

## THREE WAYS TO EXPAND YOUR INFLUENCE

Just as the best athletes use replays and coaches, you need to get more objective about the way you lead your organization, determining how you're already leading—both the good and the bad. Corrections may require less effort and hard work than the evaluation. And some corrections begin without conscious thought, once recognition is made. Here are three ways to expand your influence.

### 1. Ask "The Question of Influence"

You can learn how to expand your influence by observing that pragmatic group of workers, salespeople. A *good* salesman assumes he has 100 percent influence at the start of every sales interview. If he misses a sale, he assumes he was lacking sufficient influence that time, but still goes to the next prospect as if he has full influence.

Now travel upscale to a *great* salesman. Naturally, he

assumes he has full influence as he approaches a sale. Like the good salesman, he doesn't make every sale either. However, when the great salesman misses a sale, he doesn't assume he had too little influence. He still assumes he had 100 percent influence and figures he *made* the prospect refuse his offer.

Why does he do this? First, it's the truth. He knows he can make anything happen with his influence; he's done it before. But, second, it's a useful point of view. It doesn't pay to assume he had less than 100 percent influence. What can he learn from the situation if he assumes he had nothing to do with the missed sale? Nothing. So he asks himself, "What did I do, or not do, to make that prospect *not* buy?"

By asking himself that question, he learns about himself. That's the most important person for him to know about. Great salesmen often ask the people who didn't buy to tell them why. This is more than just a sales technique; it's a chance to see the sales call on instant replay. If salespeople can get the truth, they can discover how to be successful next time.

Of course, the great salesman also asks himself what he did to make the prospect *buy*. He assumes the success was due to his 100 percent influence, not due to chance. This way he continues to learn about himself and his influence, and he has the opportunity to grow.

What about you, the manager? What do you do when something goes wrong? Do you assume you had 100 percent influence? Take a tip from the great salesperson and assume you made it happen (or not happen). Ask yourself:

## THE QUESTION OF INFLUENCE

### WHAT DID I DO (OR NOT DO)
### TO MAKE THIS HAPPEN (OR NOT HAPPEN)?

Suppose you've just had a meeting with your staff to introduce a new idea you feel very strongly about. You explained it well and did everything you could to convince them of your idea's merit, knowing that if they didn't feel enthusiastic about it they wouldn't implement it with the spirit needed for success.

However, they received it in a lukewarm way although willing to do whatever you want. They didn't grab onto it as if it were their own project. You realize that you've failed to get your desired result—their enthusiastic support. This valuable idea will go down the drain because your staff didn't buy it and you can't push it through without their energies.

You can go back to your office now and figure out all the ways your staff is bad at accepting new ideas, how they always throw cold water on your hot ideas. You can even go to one of your staff members who seemed interested and complain about the others. This may make you feel better, but it won't help you make the future different. Instead, you can ask yourself The Question of Influence and start to learn more about yourself—and how *you* made them feel lukewarm. What did you do, or not do, and what can you do differently next time?

---

## MBI ACTIONS

**#8.** Recall a project where everything fell into place but the reason is a mystery to you. After all, if you don't know what you did or didn't do to make it happen, how will you repeat your success? Run through the events in your own mind while applying The Question of Influence. Figure out what you did, unconsciously, that made it work out.

**#9.** Focus on an issue that isn't working out. Ask yourself The Question of Influence so you can be objective about what you've done or not done to make this happen. When you determine the answer, alter your behavior and watch the effect. Pick a simple matter so you can observe a quick reversal and learn more about your influence.

## 2. Take a Useful Point of View

Asking yourself The Question of Influence, even when you're convinced you had no influence in the matter, brings you to the second way to expand your influence: taking a useful point of view. Ask yourself The Question of Influence because you know the truth: YOU CAN NEVER NOT LEAD. Even if you don't recognize it at the moment, it's the truth. Discipline yourself to take this point of view.

People take a point of view by habit. Whatever that point of view is, it's not something they were born with—it's an outlook acquired by habit. Maxwell Maltz, in *Psycho-Cybernetics,* reveals that most people don't take responsibility for their habits, acting as if they can't change them. He says it takes twenty-one days of conscious effort to take on a new habit. After that, your new habit continues unconsciously, replacing the old one.[2]

---

### — MBI ACTIONS —

**#10.** Train yourself to use The Question of Influence. Train yourself to take the useful point of view that you have 100 percent influence. Do this for twenty-one days so it will become a new habit. You'll be pleased with the results.

Put a note on your calendar to think about The Question of Influence in the morning and after lunch. Put a sign on your desk facing you. Tell your colleagues that you're doing it, and ask them to remind you.

---

After you've gained the habit of taking this responsible point of view, you'll find how useful it is as a key to opening doors that seemed locked. Use it like a drowning man grasping for a straw. Even if you can't see how you could possibly have influenced a matter, ask yourself, "What did I do (or not do) to make this happen (or not happen)?"

It's useless to assume you had no influence. It means

your organization is out of your control. It also means you're helpless to make it work the way you want. Leadership is the total effect you have on the people and events around you. You can become a more effective leader by taking conscious responsibility for your influence.

### 3. Use Those Around You As Your Mirror

Many times you will ask yourself The Question of Influence and not know the answer. At these times, you can reach for the third way to expand your influence: using the people around you as your mirror. Ask those involved or those who can observe you objectively, "What did I do (or not do) to make this happen (or not happen)?"

For example, if you've delegated a task and find it undone, you might ask the person to whom you've delegated it, "Can you tell me what I did, or didn't do, that caused you to not get the task done? I'm not asking what *you* could have done better, but what *I* could have done better." As you ask others for feedback, you'll learn about yourself. And as you do this, you'll be leading others to imitate your sense of self-responsibility by looking to their own actions, not the actions of others, to explain success or failure.

Don't pass up this opportunity to learn more about what you do well. You can grow by realizing your unconscious strengths too, not just your unconscious weaknesses. On a job well done, you might acknowledge someone for his or her part in the success and then ask, "What did I do, or not do, to make it easier for you to achieve success?" Get all the feedback you can, just as the great salesperson does.

Rouse executive Bruce Alexander recognizes that feedback is always available if you keep yourself tuned in. For example, he recalls, "Certainly the point that you can never not lead has real value for me—the notion that everything you do has an impact on people. And I've had reactions. One day, one of my managers said to me, 'Boy, you really seem down.' I was chairing a meeting of the divisional group, and I was concerned over something that had happened on one of the jobs. I had to catch myself.

"As I go into a meeting now with the divisional staff, I say to myself that if something untoward has happened on one of our jobs, I cannot afford to carry it into the meeting and share it. With all the other projects going on, I can't have people feel that the leadership of the division is not upbeat. It's just remarkable how much people react even to facial expressions. They are much more important than I would ever have imagined. I'm always careful now about what my demeanor is saying."

---

Is this easy to do? For most people, no. But that gives you some idea of the hard work and effort involved in being objective with yourself. When you discover from your own observation and from feedback that your influence was greater than you had imagined, you can start to make accommodations. This may mean better listening, clearer instructions, more favorable words for a job well done, or confronting situations that you normally like to avoid. There may be times you'll need to step out of character for the good of your organization. Chapter 3 will show you how to lead yourself and others to be open to change.

By the way, most managers are not good at taking responsibility for the *good* things that happen. It's just as important to find out how your influence makes things happen right. After all, you want to encourage that from yourself. For example, suppose that meeting with your staff had gone the other way, and they had jumped on your new idea like a dog on a bone. Don't sit back and think you were just lucky this time or that your staff must have been in a good frame of mind. Ask yourself The Question of Influence to see what you did well. And if you're still not sure, ask them— they're experts on you.

```
┌──────────────── MBI ACTIONS ────────────────┐
│                                              │
│  #11. Look at a situation that's going       │
│  wrong and you have no idea why it's         │
│  turning out that way. Use The Question      │
│  of Influence to review the happenings.      │
│  Visualize the events and "watch" yourself   │
│  to find a clue. Keep focused on what        │
│  you've done and said, on how you've         │
│  looked. But also recall what you haven't    │
│  done or said, or how you haven't looked.    │
│  Bring together the other people who are     │
│  involved to ask them how they view the      │
│  matter. Ask them what you did or didn't     │
│  do to cause the present outcome and what    │
│  you might do to change it.                  │
│                                              │
│      Pay particularly close attention to     │
│  those areas where you're normally unaware   │
│  of yourself and your actions—for example,   │
│  your facial expression. As you know,        │
│  people read each other's faces all the      │
│  time. They look for more than what they     │
│  see; they look for what they don't see.     │
│  The lack of a "look of approval" can be     │
│  read as disapproval.                        │
│                                              │
│      Go back to the people involved to       │
│  correct the erroneous message that was      │
│  received (unless it wasn't erroneous, and   │
│  you need to reconsider your own motives      │
│  and desires).                               │
│                                              │
└──────────────────────────────────────────────┘
```

## SEVEN TIPS FOR BUILDING YOUR INFLUENCE

To ease the path of self-evaluation and the growth that follows, consider the following lessons. Take courage from these tips because your potential worst enemy on the path is you. Throughout this book, as you read the cases and analogies, consider this: if it's already been done, it's possible. Take a positive attitude toward your ability to enhance your leadership.

### 1. Learn a Lesson From Lombardi and Make Every Action Count

Vince Lombardi is remembered for his authoritarian approach to coaching, but his understanding of the subtleties of influence is often overlooked. For example, he told a team official about a trade he had made. "I just got rid of a helluva good football player." When asked why he did that, Lombardi replied, "Well, I'll tell you. I don't want any bad apples in my organization. I get one apple in the bushel over here and the rest will start rotting, too." The player he got rid of was a great player and All-Pro. As much as he would suffer without the services of an All-Pro, Lombardi knew that keeping this "bad apple" would make a mockery of all he preached, and the team couldn't afford that.

When asked why he was so hard, he answered, "I was hired here to produce winning football teams, and that's what I'm going to produce. I don't hold malice about them [the players] sneaking out, but I can't afford to let one go because then the rest are going to go." He didn't say the rest *might* go, he said they *would* go. Lombardi knew that what he did, or didn't do, *made* things happen, not just allowed things to happen.[3]

---

## MBI ACTIONS

**#12.** Recall a minor violation of your authority that you let slip by. Ask The Question of Influence to determine the impact this had on major matters in your organization. If you see that it had a big impact, take actions to correct the minor issue and watch for a correlative change in the major situation.

---

### 2. Do You Need to Change?

What about you? Do you need to borrow from Lombardi to become a better leader? No and yes. No: you don't need to take on his style. Yes: you do need to take the personal responsibility he took for the results of his team. Vince Lombardi was a great salesman, and he always assumed he had 100 percent influence, even when things were going poorly.

Lombardi's acceptance of the full extent of his influence was no different from Beverly Patley's when she accepted her role in the Sunday customer service problem at Quality Markets.

The value of The Question of Influence is in its usefulness. And you can't judge that until you've used it. As Maltz says, it takes twenty-one days to learn a new habit. Give yourself that long to begin using The Question habitually. Once it's second nature to assume 100 percent influence, you'll have your own mirror with you all the time. Make it a habit to begin asking yourself The Question with every piece of news and with every happening that confronts you. It will become an instant replay for you.

You'll discover that The Question of Influence—*What did I do (or not do) to make this happen (or not happen)?*— brings answers right back to you, and brings matters under your control.

As you start to get a greater feeling for the full extent of your influence, you'll discover more leadership within yourself. You'll learn about you, not about others. You'll see the impact of the look on your face, the tone of your voice, your ability to give instructions, and every other behavior. You'll find subtleties that you hadn't recognized. And these discoveries will lead you to make changes in yourself very naturally. The only thing that might block your progress is you.

### 3. Don't Limit Yourself by Your Past

To look at this possible block, consider an experiment with a pike and some minnows. Pikes and minnows have a well-defined relationship: pikes eat minnows.

In this experiment, a pike was placed in a large fish tank with a bunch of minnows. Guess what he did? He ate the minnows, all of them. Then a bell jar was placed over the pike and later more minnows were put into the tank.

The pike tried to eat the minnows but kept banging his nose against the bell jar. After doing this for a while, he quit trying to get the minnows. Later he tried again. But he got his nose hurt without getting any chow, so he stopped. After a few more tries, the pike stopped going after the minnows at all, even though he was hungrier than ever.

The experimenters then took the bell jar out of the tank. The pike still didn't go after the minnows, even though they now swam right in front of him. The pike had made a decision: if he tried to eat, he would only wind up with a hurt nose and no food, so there was no point in trying. The pike went belly up, dead from lack of food despite the minnows swimming all around him.

What had been a legitimate decision at first became a wrong decision later. People do this, too. The moral: At each moment you need to consider that you may have a power different from what you had in the past. *You* may be different, *the others involved* may be different, *the time and circumstances* may be different.

For example, a manager we'll call Doug Peters learned to speak with great force when he was starting his career in construction. He did it to make up for a lack of expertise. Twenty years later, during a period of self-evaluation, he realized that his years of experience had now brought him credibility so he could speak more gently and still be respected. In fact, his earlier force had alienated many people from him. They were afraid of his gruffness.

What had been useful to Peters twenty years ago was now working against him. Like the pike, he had made a valid decision but neglected to observe the potential for new behavior at a later time, even though he knew the original behavior had kept a distance between himself and others. When Peters decided to ease up, the result was a new image that opened communication. A new moment had brought with it a new potential. Only this manager's previous lack of self-awareness had limited his ability to move on.

### Self-Check

*Investigate where you are acting like a prisoner of your past:*

> *—What actions or habits of mine were
> useful once but are no longer
> appropriate?*

*—What issues in my organization have I abandoned in the past that I can now approach with a new understanding of my influence?*

*—What situations that I have been trying to change or just live with—based on my old point of view of my influence—now bear new evaluation?*

Don't be like the pike. By using The Question of Influence and acknowledging that you can never not lead, you'll be different everyday. You'll be discovering more about yourself. You'll see decisions you made in the past about your influence that were perfectly valid then, but are no longer realistic and shouldn't guide your actions today. Each new moment has a new potential.

---

## MBI ACTIONS

**#13.** List three decisions you've made about your leadership which you now recognize are no longer appropriate and are therefore limiting you. Train yourself to new actions.

**#14.** Make a note on your calendar for next Monday to review your progress and look for more places to enhance your use of influence. Do this for four weeks.

---

### 4. You Were Born With Enough Leadership Ability

Once you recognize that you can never not lead, and work from that point of view, your innate leadership will always be enough: 100 percent. While you will remain unconscious of your impact much of the time, you can always return to The Question of Influence as a context for objectivity and self-evaluation.

Your next job becomes developing the humility and courage to find and examine your links to the workplace you manage. This is just as applicable to your marriage or to being a parent.

While the experience may humble you, it will also excite you and provide a freshness on the job which kindles enthusiasm. You can then bring this enthusiasm back to the workplace and influence others to have the same verve, which in turn feeds you. Definitely an upward-bound spiral of influence. You were born with enough leadership ability. MBI enables you to find more of it and use it.

### 5. You Can't Delegate Your Responsibility

A successful saleswoman started her own company selling office equipment, call her Michelle Kelly of A-Plus Office Automators in Atlanta. After one year she had succeeded in maintaining her own high sales volume and had two others selling. She appointed her secretary as office manager.

Two years later, the A-Plus sales staff was up to five and the administrative staff had two employees, including the company's fourth office manager. The first manager, the secretary, had sunk in over her head; Kelly was able to return her to the secretarial position. But then, no matter how good things looked at first, each office manager Kelly hired ran into trouble with the salespeople and was unable to keep the administration effective.

Kelly couldn't understand it. She had given each manager responsibility over everyone in the company, and the most recent one, Tracey, had been successful in another company as business manager. Now Tracey was going the way of the rest. Whereas Michelle Kelly had previously pointed a finger at the managers she had hired, she now felt she should point it at herself. It was time to ask herself The Question of Influence: "What did I do (or not do) to make this happen (or not happen)?"

She met with Tracey and asked her, "Do you recognize that your office management has not been successful?" Tracey agreed. Kelly went on, "Please, let's talk this out so I can find out what I'm doing to cause this. I'm satisfied that you have what it takes to be an office manager. I know I'll never find someone who can do the job until I figure out what I've been doing to make it impossible for an office manager to succeed."

As Michelle Kelly and Tracey talked, Kelly saw that she had wanted to pass more to Tracey than just the office manager's authority. She wanted to pass on her own responsibility as president of the company. While Kelly retained the power to hire, fire, and review pay for the sales staff, she wanted to hold Tracey responsible for their performance, such as putting in enough hours of work, following up leads, making calls after installation to ensure satisfaction, obtaining referrals, and complying with all the systems Kelly had devised for A-Plus. This way, Kelly could devote her time to selling and not have to deal with the part of the business that she really didn't like or feel good at, the supervising and disciplining of employees.

But the sales staff resented and ignored Tracey's supervision. They knew where the real power was—Michelle Kelly was the boss. And as boss, she was acting as if she didn't have to be responsible for her job. Hence, others acted the same way.

Kelly recognized that she had looked the other way when the sales staff ignored policies. She had hoped Tracey would bring them in line and chided the office manager when nothing happened. Now Kelly saw that Tracey could never get it done because Tracey wasn't the president: Michelle Kelly was the president *acting* as if she wasn't. This meant the company was working without a boss. A-Plus lacked direction, certainty, and discipline.

When Kelly came to grips with this, she called a staff meeting of all employees and apologized for the mess she had made. She re-assigned Tracey as office manager, with functional authority over all administrative matters. She told the sales staff she had directed Tracey to collect and keep certain records that she would review. She, Kelly, would supervise the sales staff's work, although Tracey would often be watching things for Kelly so that she could still devote time to selling.

Privately, Kelly asked the sales staff how they'd like to be supported by her and how they felt in the past. She was astounded to find that four of the five salespeople were so displeased with her lack of leadership that they were looking elsewhere for work. But, with her new realization of her responsibility, they were ready for a new beginning at A-Plus. The last salesman said he liked the lack of supervision and he quit, much to the relief of everyone else in the company.

---

You can delegate your authority to others, and ask them to be responsible for its use. But you can never delegate your responsibility for what they do with your authority: it's still yours, and you're still responsible for it.

---

## MBI ACTIONS

**#15.** Pick a delegation you've made that isn't going well. Apply The Question of Influence to see if you've abdicated your responsibility for the results. Involve the person you delegated so you can learn more, making sure he or she understands that the inquiry is about your leadership, not the employee's "followership."

---

### 6. How to Lead by Accident

In basketball, the guard's position is normally played by the smallest player on the court. When shooting, his job is to get close enough to take shots which have a high percentage of success. This can be difficult when the opposition has assigned one man to keep him away, and stationed their big men between the guard and the basket.

Consider a guard—call him Jones—who notices something about the opponents. They watch his head, shoulders and hands to judge where he's about to go. So Jones learns how to fake to the right with his head and shoulders, making his defender commit himself. He then drives toward the basket and fakes a pass to his left, pulling two other defenders in that direction.

Finally, he's already made a deal with one of his own big men to stand still, and Jones uses this man as a shield between himself and the other big defenders. So, smooth as silk, he drives toward the basket and makes an easy, high percentage layup. It's as simple as that. He's discovered and used his full influence.

Not all guards use their influence with such success. Some haven't figured out how to make the opposition move away. But that's only part of the story. Since these guards aren't without influence, their predictability and lack of offensive deception have *made* their opponents' defensive coverage excellent. They've accidentally led the opposition to play well against them. They should ask The Question of Influence: "What did I do (or not do) to make this happen (or not happen?"

———

Phil Moore, foreman of Shipping and Receiving at Steel Warehouse in South Bend, IN, made a startling discovery about his influence.

Often his boss, Plant Superintendent Larry Kahlmorgan, would tell him to get his workers to do something, perhaps space the bands more carefully on the coils they were shipping. Moore would then go into the plant and tell his crew, "Larry wants you to do a better job spacing the bands."

Moore noticed that his people were more careful about the banding when Larry was around but became careless again when Moore was the only one there. This aggravated Moore and he often complained about the crew. One day he realized that *he* might be the source of the problem. After all, he had told them *Larry* wanted them to band more carefully— and they did so whenever Larry was around.

On top of that, Phil Moore had never said he, Phil, wanted them to band more carefully. They were responding to his unconscious signals. When he was the only supervisor, they banded the easier way. He now saw that he had led them to this behavior. He made a subtle change that made all the difference.

Moore chuckled as he related, "I just changed one word in my orders. I started saying 'I want you to do this or that' instead of saying 'Larry wants you to do this or that.' You know something, they started doing what I wanted. I guess they were following my orders all along, and I was giving them the wrong orders."

Like the basketball guard who's covered like a blanket because of the unconscious leadership he provides to his opposition, Moore found he had an impact he didn't recognize.

## 7. Monitor Your Influence

Every customer complaint that comes to Giant Food's general offices comes to Alvin Dobbin, senior vice-president of Operations. He handles quite a few himself. "I'll pick up the telephone and return a customer's call. One customer shops at 2:00 A.M., and he's entitled to the same service he'd get at six in the evening. So I talk with him. We want people to know there's a tremendous sense of urgency on our part, to do the things that make us Giant."

Some of Dobbin's managers don't like his taking the complaints and ask that they be allowed to take care of the problems in their departments. "I say I appreciate the desire on their part, but they have to understand this is a way for me to get a pulse on what's happening. Some weeks I do five calls, some none, some ten. I don't take every one that comes in— just those of a significant nature or one that comes directly to me. I've told customers, 'In the future call me directly. This is my phone number; I'm in my office. Let me know whether we get better or worse.'

"I have a little old lady who calls at least once a month. She called the other day and said, 'I've baked some bread for you, and I'd like you to go by the store where I shop to pick it up.' That makes it all worthwhile. When she first called, she was angry at Giant, and now she's a big fan."

Dobbin feels this is one important way he can personally ensure the service in all the stores. By doing this he sets a standard of involvement consistent with that promoted by CEO Izzy Cohen. He knows what's going on in the stores, he demonstrates humility to his top managers, he keeps store managers vitally concerned about the well-being of their customers, and he retains the right to act like someone who's involved in the trenches, someone who cares.

## NINE VARIATIONS ON THE QUESTION OF INFLUENCE

The Question of Influence is, *What did I do (or not do) to make this happen (or not happen)?* While these particular words ask the question precisely, you can use any words you prefer which convey the same meaning. If you have difficulty in any given situation, consider these variations.

1. Did I follow through when I used my authority or did I look the other way, thereby giving a conflicting message?

2. If I were one of my people, how would I feel about me in this situation? What did they want or need from me?

3. Was I active or passive in this situation? What effect did my passivity have?

4. How did I really want it to turn out? Did I do whatever was needed to make that happen? Did I act as if it was a high priority to me?

5. Did my silence give consent or approval without my recognizing it? Was that counterproductive?

6. What could I have done differently? What effect would that have had?

7. Did that success happen by accident? How did I influence it? What part did I play?

8. Did my actions speak louder than my words?
9. How would I have read my behavior if I were one of my people?

## HOW TO BEST LEARN MBI AND APPLY IT TO YOUR JOB

To make the most of this book, you'll need an open mind and some goals. Your progress is confined only by unconscious self-limitations.

These limitations are like water to a fish. If you could ask a fish, "How do you like the water?" he'd reply, "Water? What's water?" If you said, "It's the stuff all around you," he'd say, "There's nothing around me." Fish don't know about water. You have certain attitudes about yourself and others that are like water to the fish. They've been with you so long that you no longer see them.

To help you help yourself down the path with minimum limitations, do the following exercise on Beginner's Mind and choose some goals for self-improvement. The only way to guarantee success is to take the learning out of the realm of intellectual behavior into real life—on the job. Then you can try out your discoveries and make them second nature. You can prove to yourself that you have new abilities. So give yourself some projects that will affect you at work.

### Use "Beginner's Mind"

A professor received a student who had been having trouble learning. The teacher poured her visitor a cup of tea. When the cup was full, she kept on pouring. The alarmed pupil watched the tea overflow until he couldn't keep quiet. "The cup's full. You can't get any more tea into it!" "Exactly," the professor said as she stopped pouring. "And, like this cup, you're full—full of your own opinions and speculations. How can I teach you unless you have room in your cup?" The student nodded with understanding. People's cups are usually filled to the brim with the obvious, with common sense, and with their subconscious conclusions and opinions about life.

Regarding leadership, your cup is full—full of your ideas about leadership, full of your thoughts and decisions about yourself and how others react to you. You have successes and failures. In your case, you have many more successes.

To enhance your leadership through self-discovery, you'll have to empty your cup. Does this mean you should forget everything you now know? No. But you can look over the "tea" in your cup to see what's still appropriate. You may want to add some or throw some away.

For example, ten years ago, you may have decided that you needed to speak loudly with force to be followed. Today that may not be true. Or the contrary may be true. In the past, you may have tried being forceful and found that people resented it. To accommodate, you may have decided to keep your mouth shut until you explode. Maybe today you can do it differently.

Your "leadership" cup is full—going all the way back to when you were a child—from every leadership role you've ever had or ever shied away from. This is a chance for you to learn more about yourself, whether you're the president of a company or manager of a department. You may find things in the past that worked but you've forgotten to continue or things you decided not to do in the past that you should start now.

You'll have a chance to suspend belief in the firm opinions you previously held and subject them to scrutiny, keeping the good ones, discarding ones that don't work, and adding others. Without being stupid, people sometimes don't learn something new because they're blinded by what they already know.

To be open to learning each moment of life, you can strive to observe life with an empty cup—with a "beginner's mind."

Think how it feels to be brand new to something—a new place or new food or new job. You've never seen it or done it before, so you look at it carefully. If you could watch yourself in your present job with a beginner's mind, you could continuously use The Question of Influence. As you discover how you're linked to the effects around you—using the point of view that you have 100 percent influence—you will naturally make corrections, consciously and unconsciously. Since you are already committed to doing the best work you can, the only thing stopping you from doing better is that you don't know what more to do. Beginner's Mind can help you learn.

## Exercise Your Beginner's Mind

Pour yourself a glass of juice and go to a quiet, private place where you can take twenty minutes undisturbed. Put the glass of juice down in front of you, close your eyes for a moment, and open your eyes to the glass as if you've never seen one before and never tasted juice.

Now reach out slowly, noticing everything about yourself. For instance, you may notice that as you reach out, your mouth starts to react even though you've only started thinking about it. Notice that you monitor the movement of your hand and that the glass has a feel to it that you haven't noticed in years. As you lift it, you may be surprised by the weight.

Bring it to your mouth, noticing that you watch it as it comes, feeling the cup first against one lip and then against the other. Even before it enters your mouth, you feel the temperature and pressure of the glass. When did you last notice that?

You'll be amazed at the number of sensations you've taken for granted. Things occur around you, but you're no longer aware of them. Isn't this like going to work? Isn't this the way you observe yourself—same old stuff?

All this has happened and you haven't even drunk the juice yet. If you take the time to fully experience all that's happening, you've already taken longer than you usually take to drink the entire glass.

Now, start to pour the juice into your mouth, noticing how it runs around the floor of your mouth, causing your mouth to shout to your brain, sending messages of tingles, temperature, texture. The juice may lose its taste in a concurrent wave of messages to your sensation centers.

Drinking like this can take a long time. You might even find a new way to take pleasure from food with less intake. Can you imagine eating a pizza with a beginner's mind—or your favorite food?

Keep it up, even noticing that the entire freshness of the Beginner's Mind experience is starting to fade. You've already started to lose the ability to do Beginner's Mind with a beginner's mind.

Why do this? To revitalize your ability to observe your influence. To recognize how much you do unconsciously. To see how easy it can be to take a new look if only you're willing to come in with an empty cup.

This doesn't mean that all the knowledge you have is useless. To the contrary, you're already a professional. But by taking a new point of view, in a new moment of time, you'll be able to see further into the full potential of your ability to lead: 100 percent influence.

How do you achieve Beginner's Mind on the job? Make a plan to ask yourself The Question of Influence: "What did I do (or not do) to make this happen (or not happen)?" Ask it in a systematic way. Put it in your daily planner. Make yourself a sign. Put it on your management checklists. Ask your people until you hear them asking each other, and asking you.

As a start, do this exercise with Beginner's Mind, even if you don't usually do things like this. Do it for the good of your company. Remember the pike and the minnows, and commit yourself to leading as if each new moment has a new potential.

---

### MBI ACTIONS

**#16.** Make a list of five specific improvements you wish to achieve in your leadership. Use real situations from work where possible. Attack your main problems and also attack situations you're just putting up with. Use these goals as workshop projects to apply the discoveries you make and the tools you learn from *Managing*

*By Influence.* Not only will it encourage you to try things out, but it will take the learning beyond being an intellectual experience to becoming second nature.

We expect that much of what you try to remember about this book will be forgotten, but that which becomes second nature—part of your unconscious leadership—will stay with you forever.

Review yourself weekly. This will keep your job challenging and growing.

## HOW ONE COMPANY PRESIDENT USED EMPLOYEE FEEDBACK TO MEASURE HIS INFLUENCE

A bed manufacturer, call it Sleepwell Products of Seattle, had a production line that had been turning out fifty units per day for years. After reading some articles on quality circles, the company president, Lew Weinberger, started them at Sleepwell and Production Group 3 implemented several new methods that they devised in their quality circle meetings. Production jumped to an average of sixty-four units per day.

Weinberger was thrilled and started a bonus system to reward the employees for their high production. Everyone was happy. After several months, two members of the same group came up with some exceptional ideas that pushed production even higher, to seventy-eight units per day with the same labor. The ideas also were applicable to other production problems the company had been having, and the result was an increase in productivity throughout. Weinberger was elated and gave the two employees an extra bonus.

Shortly thereafter, for no apparent reason, production on line 3 dropped back to fifty-nine units and several members asked to be transferred to other groups. A couple were on the verge of quitting.

Fortunately for Lew Weinberger and Sleepwell, he had the good sense to ask himself The Question of Influence. Unfortunately, he didn't know what he had done to bring this about. At wit's end, he decided to ask help from the only people who could give it: the workers of Production Group 3.

He called a meeting and said, "I need your help. You've given it to me before, and I need it now. Please tell me what I've done to ruin the spirit of your group."

The people were quiet at first, but they opened up little by little to reveal Weinberger's influence. When the first increase happened, he had rewarded the group and that went well. But, when the second ideas came out of the quality circle meetings, he had rewarded the two people who came up with the ideas. The others resented it, and even the two who got the bonuses felt strange and isolated from their group. They all started to get on each other's nerves, and the feeling of family that had previously helped them work out their differences disappeared. The two who got the bonuses didn't want to appear ungrateful, so they just kept quiet.

Lew Weinberger now had his instant replay. With new insight, he apologized to the group and gave some minor bonuses to other quality circle members. Everything fell into place again. He also learned to consider Production Group 3 as his partners on all issues affecting them.

He could easily have pointed his finger at the crew or at fate, but he knew that YOU CAN NEVER NOT LEAD. He accepted this point of view even though he couldn't see by himself how he was involved.

## THE QUESTION OF INFLUENCE

### WHAT DID I DO (OR NOT DO)
### TO MAKE THIS HAPPEN (OR NOT HAPPEN)?

---

## MBI ACTIONS

**#17.** Use The Question of Influence when you're with other people. Verbalize it, like thinking out loud. Let others observe the thought process you use and recognize your willingness to assume responsibility. Watch to see how this leads others to take the same attitude. Be pleased with how much they are influenced by you. Use The Question by design so it will become completely spontaneous for you.

---

# 3

# How to Lead People to Change

A Chinese proverb tells us: "If we keep going the way we're going, we're likely to wind up where we're headed." That's okay if you're still headed the same way. However, companies often keep going the way they have been going even though they're now headed someplace new.

Jim Hodges became senior vice-president of the Trust Department of a bank in Philadelphia. He was new to the bank and was fortunate to have on his staff a supervisor, Grace, who had forty-four years of service with the department. Whenever Hodges had a question about the history of some policy or procedure, he had only to ask Grace.

One day he asked her when a certain minor policy was implemented and she answered, "I don't know. They were doing that when I came here."

Can you imagine any policy or procedure remaining the same for more than forty-four years? Considering the changes in modern business, that's remarkable. As you might expect, the policy was awkward at best. It was easy for Hodges, a beginner at the bank, to spot it. But people had worked around it for many years—and done it successfully as proven by the bank's excellent record of service.

Why do people work around situations they know don't meet their needs? Most often, it's because they accept them as permanent or "given" and don't think change is possible.

## UNDERSTANDING CHANGE

At first, most people react negatively to change. It seems to be an unconscious part of their personalities. But change is as essential in business as in life itself.

Physical life would be over without change. Virtually your whole body changes, cell by cell, over a period of seven years. You're not more than seven years old. The universe is built on change and motion.

As a manager, your job is to lead your people to whatever change is needed. Major change is often desirable and possible. A caterpillar can learn to walk fast or even to jog, but the big difference comes when it transforms into a butterfly.

The starting place for this type of change is you. Use your Beginner's Mind and find out where you've been jogging instead of flying.

## BREAKING THROUGH YOUR LEADERSHIP LIMITS

To be able to lead your people and your organization to change, you must first observe your own attitudes toward the past. Many of these attitudes are unconscious and unchallenged.

Most managers, most of the time, treat the happenings of the past as if they were the permanent or given nature of things, rather than simply things that occurred in the past.

For example, if Jim and Fred haven't worked well with each other in the past, people typically say, "That's just the way they are. Everyone knows about Jim and Fred. It's their nature—they just don't get on well together."

Or if quality and production have been off every summer in your company for the last six years, you might say, "That's just the way it is during summer in our company. It's caused by vacations and the vacation attitudes of the people. It's just the nature of our business. We've come to expect it."

Or if you haven't been able to delegate authority well in the past, you say, "I'm just not good at delegating authority. Really, it's just my way. My people and I work around it. I guess it's my nature or personality."

You say these things rather than comment, "In the past, Jim and Fred haven't worked well together." Or, "In the past, quality and production have been off in the summer." Or, "In the past, I haven't delegated my authority well."

By considering the behavior of the past to be the permanent nature of the situation, your underlying assumption is that it won't be any different in the future. And, if you assume the future will be only an extension of the past, what will you do to change it? Nothing.

Since you can never not lead, your lack of action to change events does more than just permit them to continue—it *leads* them to continue.

In your unconscious mind-set, your unrecognized attitude about most of life is: that's the nature of things; that won't change; that's a given. Jim and Fred will always be at odds; the company will always have production trouble in the summer; I'll always be bad at delegating (Lord knows, I've tried!).

Regarding leadership, this point of view becomes a self-fulfilling prophesy. You act in a way that's true to your attitude. In terms of managing by influence, you are leading to a future which merely extends the past. The problem is, you usually point your finger at the circumstances instead of at yourself, the boss. The ability to lead people to be open to change requires using The Question of Influence.

---

## MBI ACTIONS

**#18.** List five situations that you're putting up with because you don't think they can be changed. Determine for each one how your apparent acceptance of the issue has led to its continuance. Use The Question of Influence.

---

### HOW A COMPANY PRESIDENT LED HIS PEOPLE TO CHANGE

Jeff Peck was pleased with the success of his young company, call it Simon Services Corporation of Oakland, CA. Si-

mon Services had grown dramatically in the grounds maintenance business in the past four years, with profits, quality, and
personnel all falling into place. Although he had several key
managers who could be counted on, he regularly had to inter-
vene in issues involving one of the project managers, Jim, and
the manager of maintenance, Fred.

Every time Peck considered implementing new systems
and procedures, he had to skirt around the poor relationship
between Jim and Fred. In addition, since these managers
were so important to Simon Services, their inability to work
in harmony soured the rest of the company and set an example for behavior that Peck didn't want.

Each would complain to Peck about the other, and he was
unsure what to do about the situation. Then he considered
matters in light of having 100 percent influence. Jeff Peck
reviewed his own attitude about Jim and Fred, and decided
that the only useful point of view was to assume that he, not
Jim or Fred, was the source of the problem. He also needed to
discard his old attitude that they would never change, that
that's just the way they are.

Jeff Peck restated the problem. Instead of thinking, "Jim
and Fred just don't work well together," he considered, "In the
past, Jim and Fred have not worked well together. How do I
want the future to be? What have I done or not done to make
it this way in the past?" Then he took action. First, he met
with Jim.

*Peck:* "Jim, do you recognize that you and Fred haven't
worked well together in the past?"

*Jim:* "Of course, everyone knows that."

*Peck:* "Is that okay with you, or would you rather work
better with him?"

*Jim:* "I'd like to get on with him, but he's hard to work
with and won't change."

*Peck:* "Would you meet him halfway?"

*Jim:* "Yes, but he won't."

*Peck:* "Would you be willing to try to have a better relationship if he would?"

*Jim:* "Yes, but he won't."

*Peck:* "If he's willing, would you be willing to sit down with him and me to make a new start?"

*Jim:* "Yes."

*Peck:* "When we do that, may I tell him what you've said?"

*Jim:* "Yeah, I guess so. He probably knows how I feel anyway. And I'd really like things to get better."

Then Peck met with Fred. The conversation went much the same. So Peck arranged a meeting with the two managers.

*Peck:* "I've met with you both, and you have both said you recognize that you haven't worked together well in the past. Right?"

Both said yes.

*Peck:* "And you each would like to have it be better in the future."

Both mumbled, "I would."

*Peck:* "And neither of you thinks the other will change."

Jim and Fred looked at each other and nodded their affirmation.

*Peck:* "You each said you'd be willing to meet the other halfway. Is that right?"

*Jim:* "Yes, I will."

*Fred:* "I will, too."

*Peck:* "And neither of you thought the other would be willing, right?"

Both managers smiled, nodding.

*Peck:* "Jim, Fred, you both told me you'd be willing to start new. Neither of you has trusted the other enough to work together in the past, but now here we are. Are you both willing to make it work?"

*Jim:* "Like I told you, Jeff, I'll do it."

*Fred:* "You can count on me to do my best."

*Peck continued:* "That's great. And from now on, you can both count on me to work with you. I know that I've contributed to the difficulties you've had by not sitting down like this earlier." (Jim and Fred both agreed.) "I won't tolerate it in the future. I sold you both short because I thought you'd never change. I've learned a lesson, and I know it's my job to have you two working well together, for the good of the company."

———

Jeff Peck worked through four critical points. First, he recognized his own responsibility for Jim and Fred's poor relationship. It's not enough to recognize that he *allowed* them to remain the same; he's the boss, so he had *led* them to stay the same by his inaction.

Second, he saw that he had assumed he couldn't change them, either because they were unwilling to change or because he wasn't good at dealing with this type of situation. This had stopped him from taking any action in the past. Jim and Fred didn't work it out by themselves because of their own mind-set about themselves and each other. And they felt justified to let it go on since Peck obviously knew about the difficulty, and his silence gave them approval.

Third, he realized he had acted as if Jim and Fred didn't care about their poor working relationship. Now he saw that they were as interested as he was in resolving it for their own good and for the good of the company. They had always been unhappy with the situation, but he hadn't noticed it; he had been blinded by his own displeasure with them.

Finally, he used The Question of Influence to see how he had led them to the past and how he could lead them to a new future.

———

What was the lesson for Jeff Peck of Simon Services? There was bad news and good news. Bad news: He was the one keeping everything stuck in the old ways. All the changes he wanted to implement were being held up by his own worst enemy—his own unconscious attitudes. But the good news: All the changes he wanted to make could be accomplished by dealing with his best friend—his new ability to observe himself as boss.

If he could change himself, he could lead the entire company to change. In the past, Peck was stopped by his own mind-set about his personal limitations, feeling he couldn't resolve personnel problems like Jim's and Fred's. Now he saw it wasn't his nature, but just the way he'd acted in the past. Peck had a new attitude about himself. He used his mirror— The Question of Influence: *What have I done (or not done) to keep things from changing?*

---

## MBI ACTIONS

**#19.** If you have two people who have not worked well together, use The Question of Influence to see how your behavior or attitude has been keeping them stuck in their old actions. Then re-read the above story, determine how you could influence your people to change, and try it. It works!

---

### THE CHANGE TRIANGLE: THREE TECHNIQUES TO BRING ABOUT EXCEPTIONAL CHANGE

The Change Triangle is a set of three techniques, each relating to a key concept in leading people to be open to change. When understood and used in combination, they provide Managing By Influence leverage, producing dramatic results from small, skillful actions.

Each technique of The Change Triangle has a dual meaning. It's both the label given to the technique *and* the key words needed to apply it.

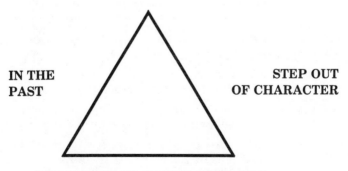

IN THE PAST          STEP OUT OF CHARACTER

FOR THE GOOD OF THE COMPANY

The purpose of The Change Triangle is to lead people to be open to change. It permits you to guide yourself and others to be willing and permissive to change. And not just small-time change, but major change in attitudes, points of view, and thought processes.

———

Mary Apperson, a dental assistant with Dr. Lloyd Moss's office in Fredericksburg, VA, found that she got upset each morning when the schedule slipped and started to erode her lunch hour. She found it hard to concentrate and hard to be her normal cheerful self. Mary attended a meeting on the issue of change, and saw that she had always considered herself to "have a short fuse," getting upset easily when things didn't go her way. And eating lunch on time was always important to her.

She also realized that when she got upset, life was harder for her and for those around her. She decided that it was time to step out of character. While she had acted this way in the past (for her entire twenty-four years, she suspected), it was time for her to find a way to work without getting so upset. If others could do it, she could too.

She committed herself to "calming down" for the good of her dental practice, her colleagues, and patients. She told the people around her that she recognized the problem and would change. They could help her by letting her know if she got grumpy. The result: they never had to! They were as pleased as Mary and as surprised at how easy it was.

What made it possible? First, Mary realized that her own assumption that she would always be easily upset was unconsciously stopping her from working to change. Like the pike, she failed to consider that every new moment had a new potential. She added the phrase "in the past" to her thoughts so she could break this attitude.

Second, she recognized that it would take a step out of character, not just a little more of the past. She would have to find a new, more potent nature within herself.

And third, Mary saw that for the good of the practice she cared so much about, she would just have to change. It was needed for something more important than her own concerns.

After a week of her new self-control, Mary was determined to carry her changed behavior into the rest of her life. She was thrilled that, after twenty-four years, she could change. She had given up on herself in the past. The change worked of course, because she now saw a new character in herself that included not being upset and changing for the better.

---

**MBI ACTIONS**

**#20.** Regarding your job, pick an unwanted characteristic about yourself, one that you've given up on the possibility of ever changing. Recognize how your limited point of view about yourself has hampered your progress. Apply The Change Triangle to yourself.

---

### Technique 1: "In the Past"

Adding the phrase "in the past" to your thoughts and conversations focuses on the assumption that the future can be different. Thinking "in the past" raises the question, "How do I want the future to be?" It may also bring to the surface your underlying feeling that, in the situation you're addressing, nothing can change—that's just the way things are. You will never consider a new potential for the future when your thought process unconsciously screens out the possibility for change. This very feeling is the block to action and it resides in your own mind, not in the situation. You can adopt a more useful point of view: that you can influence the future once you know the part you've played in the past. As the boss, you've played the major part in the past.

Jeff Peck believed it was in Jim's and Fred's nature to not work together—that was just the way they were. How did he think they'd be in the future? The same! And what was he doing to change them? Nothing! He took the attitude that they couldn't be changed. So his beliefs and actions about the two managers were consistent with his attitude. Worse yet, he didn't even recognize he had that attitude. That attitude was part of the "tea" in his leadership cup that filled the cup and blinded him from taking new actions. The breakthrough for Peck came when he said to himself, "Let me look at this as if *I've* been the source of the problem in the past, not them. And let me look at it as if I can change the way I lead them, rather than 'that's just the way I am.'"

This is the opportunity created by Beginner's Mind. By using The Question of Influence—*What did I do (or not do) to make this happen (or not happen)?*—you can create a new potential for change in your own mind. Then you'll see new demands on yourself to grow big enough in your job to handle new situations. You'll recognize that each new moment has a new potential.

Use "in the past." Begin inserting the phrase in your own thoughts as you think or talk things out with yourself in your own mind. Start adding "in the past" as you speak to people or overhear people making statements that show you they don't see a new potential.

---

"In matrix management, I was spending an enormous amount of time refereeing," says Bruce Alexander of The Rouse Company. "All the problems would come up the matrix to the top. The department heads would march into my office with problem after problem.

"Finally, I got everybody together, and essentially said, 'That's enough. You're adults. In the past I've been spending all my time refereeing, not managing, and we've got to find a way to work this out.'

"I didn't do it sooner for several reasons. First, I didn't recognize the problem until I felt extraordinary time pressures and began to look at management from the perspective of what I'm doing that's useful, productive, and contributing to good results—and what I'm doing that's not. Refereeing could be done by the managers themselves much more efficiently and effectively. While we were very effective as a division in the past, the projects Rouse was going to take on were going to make the old ways obsolete. Change was required.

"The other reason I didn't act at first was because refereeing was the pattern of management that had developed in the past. It was the status quo that everybody assumed.

"I was more direct with this set of issues than usual. I was typically more of a compromiser who dealt with things in a tactful sort of way. But there are times when subtleties and tact have to be put aside in the interests of being very direct so that everybody really understands your message. I was somewhat out of character in getting them together to make a demand on them as a group.

"They understood, and it all has worked out well. They were very open to giving me their help. Of course, my willingness to referee had led them to continue in their old habits. We have an excellent group of people at Rouse who will do whatever is needed. I only need to remember to ask. In the past, I didn't do that enough."

### Technique 2: "Step Out of Character"

Now we see the need to "step out of character"—to go beyond your usual mind-set and image of yourself to produce behavior that exceeds what was previously possible.

Stepping out of character is major change, like a caterpillar becoming a butterfly. It's the type of change dental assistant Mary Apperson made. It's the type of change Jeff Peck wanted from Jim and Fred and that Bruce Alexander wanted from his managers.

It's also the type of change Peck and Alexander needed to make in themselves so they could lead their people to step out of character.

Use "step out of character." As you recognize that the past does not need to extend into the future, ask yourself and your people to "step out of character." Don't limit yourself to demanding a linear step into the future. Shoot for a break-through step that goes beyond the old character of the situation. Find a new way to act, not just new actions within the old way. Seek a new context or framework.

To enhance your own leadership, using more of the born leader already in you, you need only step out of character and find a new possibility in yourself. Step-by-step learning is important, but it doesn't have the impact of breakthrough learning. All the techniques of management can be learned in a linear fashion, step-by-step, but that will not have the impact of simply stepping out of character further than you ever have in the past and recognizing more than ever before that you *really* are responsible for it all.

---

One of Vince Lombardi's strengths was his ability to see more in his players than even they saw in themselves. He took nothing as given. He focused on the ability in people to exceed their behavior of the past.

A statement of Lombardi's credo might have been: Give the team everything *I* know you've got. Don't stop at what *you* think you've got.

One of his All-Pros commented, "I played for three coaches before I came here. In pure knowledge of football, their level was basically the same as Lombardi's. The difference was that Lombardi got production and he got it by selling himself to us and us to ourselves. He got more out of his players. That was what put him a cut above everyone else."[1]

### Technique 3: "For the Good of the Company"

A young cashier of a firm, call it Lumber-Rite Stores of Los Angeles, was confronted one day by a customer who became very angry over an item she thought had been on special. At the checkout stand, when she was charged full price, she started talking in a loud, hostile voice, making accusations that were directed at Lumber-Rite in general, and at the cashier, Jill Janna, personally.

It happened that the customer, an older woman, reminded Janna of her least favorite aunt whom she had feared as a child. It would have been typical of Janna in her private life to either cry, be speechless, or shout at someone who talked to her this way—that's the way she had dealt with her aunt.

But at her job, Janna stood there quietly until the customer stopped for a breath. Then Janna said, with warmth and caring, "Ma'am, we just want you to be happy. From our president, David Harris, to me, we're here to make you happy. And if you thought this was still on special, I can tell you that we want you to have it at that price. I'll talk to the manager. Would that be fair enough?"

The customer's mouth dropped open. After a moment, she looked at Janna's nametag and said with a smile, "Thank you, Jill. I guess I may have been wrong—about the price, about you, and about Lumber-Rite. I appreciate the treatment and will always come back to you in the future."

When the customer left, Jill Janna asked for relief and went to the back of the store, cried for a few minutes, and then congratulated herself for doing the job the way David Harris would have done it, for the good of the store. Then she went back to work, a bigger person.

How was she able to do this? In her personal life, she would not have been able to step out of character. But at Lumber-Rite, where she considered herself to be a partner in her store and was treated like one by co-workers and management alike, she found an ability beyond her personality.

You do it, too. In business situations, you are cooperative and cordial to people whom you would not be able to get along with in your personal life. You are able to repeat instructions to people several times to be sure they understand even when you sometimes can't show the same patience with your children, spouse, or parents. You keep your work appointments better than you keep personal appointments. How come? It's a power you have to do things for a larger purpose than your own needs: for the good of the company.

*Self-Check*

*Think about your own ability to step out of character. Ask yourself:*

> *—Do I have more self-discipline at work than at home?*
>
> *—Do I accept more responsibility for my actions at work than I might at home?*
>
> *—Am I willing to do whatever is needed to get the job done, even if it's not my usual way?*

Your people have the same abilities that blossom when they are asked to change for the good of the company, because they care about the company. We'll discuss commitment to the company in depth in Chapters 6 and 7. The only reason you have a right to ask anything of your people is for the good of the company. That's why they follow your authority. But it's particularly important to recognize this basis of relationship when asking for something extraordinary.

Use "for the good of the company" (or "for the good of the agency, firm, department, practice," etc.). Say these words when you ask someone (including yourself) to step out of character. "The good of the company" is the power base of The Change Triangle. It recognizes people's deep concern for their organizations and cuts through self-imposed limitations.

---

## MBI ACTIONS

**#21.** Take your list of five situations needing change and make a plan to apply The Change Triangle techniques to two of them. Don't explain The Change Triangle, use it!

---

### TAKE A USEFUL POINT OF VIEW

In leading to change, as manager, you will gain potency when you recognize the part you've played in the past. From that point of view, you are in control of the organization you manage. Any other point of view leaves you out of control, and you can only hope for the best.

The starting point for your ability to lead to a new future is the recognition that the events of the past are no more than that. But most people assume the events of the past are the permanent nature of things. It's a more useful point of view to assume that they are merely events. For instance, our relationship with China changed in a very short time—an old assumption about the nature of things thrown out the window. It used to be that no one could run a mile in less than four minutes. And what goes up always used to come down. If you take the point of view that things can't change, you are abdicating your responsibility. Who becomes boss then? The past.

You can't change the past, or even the present. It's too late for either of those. But you can influence the future if you are willing to take the viewpoint of the great salesperson: you have 100 percent influence. Even if you can't find out how to break the past from the future in a given situation, it only makes sense to assume you had the influence.

---

### — MBI ACTIONS —

**#22.** If you find you have an item on your list which you've always felt was unchangeable, step out of character. For the good of the company, take the more useful point of view that it can be changed. Use The Question of Influence and use those around you for advice on how to apply The Change Triangle.

---

## "COMPANALITY": A WAY TO BRING OUT THE MOST IN PEOPLE

For more insight into the ability to step out of character for the good of the company, consider a special definition of the word "personality" compared to a new word, "companality."

Define "personality" as: the full expression of your individuality for the good of yourself. Consider a baby born with a full range of self-expression. There are no limits to the ability to experience and express love, happiness, fear, anger, and all the other emotions and feelings. But, as babies come into the world and begin to develop, they make decisions. For example, one baby screams and gets picked up and loved. Another one smiles and gets picked up. Both begin making decisions.

They both start with the ability to scream *and* smile, but they start forming their behavior and personality for their own personal good. In the growing-up process, they forget that they can experience and express in ways other than their own personality. In their own minds, they say, "That's the way I am, I can't change. It's just my own nature." This reinforces the behavior and proves to them that they are just that way.

The point is, by the time they are adults, people express themselves using less than their full range of abilities. They have used just enough to satisfy their own needs. While all people start out as limitless individuals, they develop more narrowly "for their own good."

The new word is "companality"—the full expression of your individuality for the good of the company. (You could substitute "agenciality," "firmality," or any word that works for your organization.) When people get involved in families, teams, or companies, they have an ability to go back to their original full range of expression and bring out those abilities which are appropriate and needed.

Take the man who saw his child run over by a car in front of his house. He ran out to find the car on his daughter's arm. Afraid to drive the car off her arm, he took hold of the bumper and lifted the car off the child. Wait a minute! A man can't lift a car. But he did, for a cause more important than his own.

Jill Janna can't confront a nasty, loud-mouthed older woman who reminds her of her aunt. But she did, for the good of the company.

And Mary Apperson was not able to control her "short fuse" all her life until she saw the need to do it for the good of her dental practice.

You and your people have the same potential to experience and express more of your innate, full individuality for the good of your company than you would for your own good. So the entry point for leading people to step out of character, and for you to step out of character, is to recognize that the past doesn't have to go on. You can make major change. You already have the ability to make major change when you act for the good of the company.

You see it in team sports all the time. That's probably the most important job for a coach in professional sports. All the teams are made up of people who have grown up as stars. The successful coach leads them to play for the good of the team, and become better for it. As was said of Vince Lombardi, "When he said, 'You were chosen to be a Packer,' he made it sound like something unique and wonderful."[2]

## *Self-Check*

*How are you at stepping out of character for the good of the company?*

> *–Think of a time you dealt with a difficult person (maybe a customer) in a difficult situation and kept your composure. Ask yourself: How does this compare with my behavior in my private life, perhaps with my family?*

> *–Remember a time at work when you surprised yourself by extending yourself past your old image, your old limitations. Ask yourself: Where did I find the drive to step out of character?*

> *–Recall an adult with whom you don't deal well in your personal life. Ask yourself: If that person were part of my company, how would I step out of character to build a better relationship?*

## EIGHTEEN VARIATIONS ON THE CHANGE TRIANGLE

Using the three phrases of The Change Triangle works in most cases. If you try them for awhile and find any of them hard to use, try these alternatives.

### IN THE PAST

Up 'til now
So far
As of now
To date
Until this moment
In previous times
Now and before
Previously

### STEP OUT OF CHARACTER

Go beyond old limits
Break with the past
Take a new outlook or point of view
Make an extraordinary (extra-ordinary) effort

### FOR THE GOOD OF THE COMPANY

For the good of us all
In the interest of the group
For the common interest
For the benefit of the organization
For the purpose of the team
Out of your concern for the company

## PUTTING THE CHANGE TRIANGLE TO USE

The power of The Change Triangle stems from its simplicity. You don't need to explain these words to anyone, they're common language. But the danger is that you won't think it's powerful, and you won't try it out. If, in the past, you might not have tried out an idea like The Change Triangle, then step out of character and give it a twenty-one-day try for the good of your company. If you don't do it, it surely won't work!

And don't explain it to people. Just go out and use the three phrases. After you've mastered these words, you can use your own.

———

As Bruce Alexander looks at his impact on The Rouse Company, he says, "I think the biggest successes have involved changing people, helping senior managers change themselves."

As he applies his influence, he assumes the most of his managers. Alexander recognizes that the future is limited by his own point of view of their past ability to change.

"Helping them bring about change in the way they approach their jobs—that's the key influence. And the other influences are fleeting at best. It's my job to demand the best of them, and have them demand the best of themselves." He can't accept people's behavior as their permanent nature. He calls on them to do whatever's needed for The Rouse Company.

---

## MBI ACTIONS

**#23.** Assign yourself a weekly project using The Change Triangle. Make a plan on Monday and check the results on Friday. Practice the techniques until they are second nature to you. Use it, don't explain it.

---

### HOW TO CHANGE SOMEONE WHO "CAN'T" CHANGE

A bank, call it National Bank of Denver, had an internal auditor, Irv, who had lost his credibility and impact in the company. His boss, Phil Dillon, vice-president of Auditing, had listened to so many lending officers talk poorly about Irv that Dillon had given up on him, referring to him as "the lonely auditor."

Irv always seemed to take an adversarial role. Furthermore, when a loan went bad and Irv had argued against it, he made sure everyone knew they had been wrong, and he had been right. This further alienated him from the others. He had done it for so long, the decision makers stopped listening to him.

No one talked with Irv anymore; only his fifteen years of service kept his job for him. Phil Dillon was a sensitive manager who recognized that although Irv was now ineffectual, he could have an important role to play, if only Irv could change his attitude and image. Everyone told Dillon to forget Irv. "He's been in that job for ten years, and you've been his boss for one year," they advised. "Let him be. You'll never change him."

After much soul searching and applying The Question of Influence, Phil Dillon decided it was his job to bring Irv into effective action. He realized that, as vice-president and Irv's boss, he was leading the auditor to continue the behavior of the past. He had been limited by his own attitude about Irv: "He'll never change, that's just his personality."

The vice-president knew that this point of view was useless, so he inserted "in the past" into his thoughts and discussions about Irv. He saw that Irv cared deeply about the company and that Irv was disturbed by his inability to help the company anymore. The boss decided that this was the lever he could use to lead his auditor to a new beginning.

Dillon approached Irv after carefully thinking out a plan.

*Dillon:* "Irv, I know how much you care about the bank. I want to discuss the role you play here. Do you recognize that you're not as effective as you could be?"

*Irv:* "What do you mean?"

*Dillon:* "In the past, people have discounted your opinion. They've stopped listening to you. Do you know that?"

*Irv:* "To some extent, they have."

*Dillon:* "To what extent?"

*Irv:* "To a great extent."

*Dillon:* "Do you agree that, in the past, you've been disregarded to an extent which is not good for the company?"

*Irv:* "Yes, I do."

*Dillon:* "In the past, Irv, I've looked the other way and let this continue. I'm now committed to seeing this change. I know how much you care about the company. I know that you're doing a job you feel needs to be done here, and you're only doing what you think best. Isn't that true?"

*Irv:* "You're the first person who's said that, Phil. I appreciate it. What you say is true, and I am frustrated."

*Dillon:* "Why do you think it's gotten this way?"

*Irv:* "Well, I usually blame it all on the others, but since we're talking straight, I suspect it must be me, too. I guess it will never change."

*Phil Dillon went on:* "Irv, just because it's been this way for awhile, doesn't mean that it can't be different in the future. In the past, you and I haven't worked on this together. You've been alone. I consider us to be partners on a project to work you back into the main flow of the company's lending process. Is that a deal?"

*Irv:* "Do you really think it's possible?"

*Dillon:* "Absolutely! Is it a deal?"

*Irv (smiling for the first time since Dillon knew him):* "It's a deal. But I don't think it's possible."

*Dillon:* "It will require something extra from you, Irv. You'll need to step out of character. You'll need to show people that you can be counted on to act for the good of the company. In the past, others have felt that you've only been acting for your own ego, and that you're a loner, not a company man."

*Irv:* "Sometimes they've been right. But usually, I've tried to do what's best for the bank. I'll do whatever is needed to get back into an influential position here. I do care, Phil. And I appreciate your coming to me. I know it took courage. Not many people come to me anymore. It's hard to take after fifteen years with the bank."

The two men devised a plan for Irv to develop a new

relationship with others, and he began carrying it out. The next day he waited for an instance when a loan analyst had done a particularly good job and he spoke up to acknowledge it. All heads turned in disbelief. Later, Irv was in disagreement with a loan being presented. In the past he would have stated his final opposition for the record and sat down unreconciled. This day, he said, "I'm still uneasy, but I'll go along with it. I believe it's at the very edge of the risk we want to take." Now, whispers ran through the loan review meeting.

After the meeting, several people came up to Irv to thank him for the part he played in the meeting. Irv told them, "In the past, I wouldn't have done what I did today. But that was the past, and I'm starting a new future."

The breakthrough occurred when Phil Dillon turned the pointing finger on himself. He recognized that his past attitude toward Irv had stopped him from leading Irv to a new relationship with his colleagues. Not only was he not leading Irv to a new relationship, he was also leading Irv to retain the past behavior and his old self image.

Nor had he acted as if Irv cared about the bank, even after fifteen years of service. When he went to Irv and acknowledged him for his commitment to the company, the words moved Irv to a new trust—so Dillon had the right to ask for extraordinary actions from Irv, for the good of the company. Irv was able to step out of character and break the cycle. Once it started, it was easy to maintain. Now Phil Dillon beams whenever he tells the story of Irv, the ex-lonely auditor.

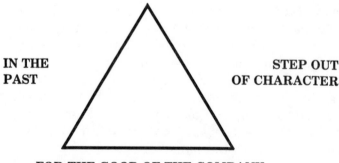

IN THE                                      STEP OUT
PAST                                        OF CHARACTER

FOR THE GOOD OF THE COMPANY

## MBI ACTIONS

**#24.** Take an instance that you've been putting up with. Think about it while saying to yourself, "in the past." If your mind replies, "That's the way it is, and that's the way it's going to stay," then you've found the real block. As Pogo, the comic strip possum, says, "We have met the enemy, and they are us."

Take a new point of view: Focus on other people's desires to change. Begin by seeking concurrence from the others that, in the past, this problem has existed. Let them know of your commitment to change and ask for theirs, even if they didn't think it was possible in the past. The worst that can happen is that things won't change. On the other hand, if you do nothing, you can be sure they won't.

# 4

# Manage the Climate to Master Your Influence

Vince Lombardi didn't have time to take care of everyone who was suffering an injury. He often went into the training room saying, "Nobody's hurt here," and everybody would get up off the tables and walk out. They got better right away.[1] Lombardi created the environment and he knew it. If he had walked through and said nothing, he would have been giving another message, one he didn't want to give.

He could have dealt with each player individually, but he had more leverage by managing the climate of the entire training room, changing it from one of *Too hurt to play* to *Playing hurt*. Each player worked out his own situation in the new climate.

Just as managing the greenhouse environment gives the horticulturist leverage over all the plants within, managing the climate of the organization gives the manager leverage over all the operations within. Climate means the prevailing temper or environmental condition.

## THREE CRITICAL FACTS ABOUT THE CLIMATE

To exercise leverage in leading, you must understand three simple but critical facts about the climate. While they are not surprising, they are normally overlooked. Don't be fooled by their simplicity.

1. **There is *always* a climate in your organization.** By definition, there is no time when a climate or environment or atmosphere does not exist. There may be many times when you do not know what the climate is, but one always exists nonetheless.

2. **The climate *always* affects everybody and everything they do.** Just as the atmosphere in the greenhouse affects everything in it, the climate of your organization affects all it touches, and it touches all. Different people or departments may overcome the climate, but they still experience its effect.

3. **You *always* affect the climate, by what you do and don't do.** Whether you realize it or not, you are always making a difference to the climate. Everyone in the organization is, but as leader, you have the primary role. While you may be reasonably aware of what you *do* to affect the climate, most leaders are much less aware of what they *don't* do to affect it. Furthermore, while most "aware" managers normally see the impact they make in a given incident, they often neglect their impact on the climate.

If you recognize these three facts, you can lead more effectively. Leadership is the total effect you have on the people and events around you. Effective leading is being consciously responsible for the total effect you have. If you don't recognize these simple truths, your effectiveness in getting your job done will suffer.

### HOW A DATA PROCESSING MANAGER INTEGRATES HIS PEOPLE INTO THE COMPANY

A pharmacy chain, call it Drug Mart of Miami, had always been a leader in computer operations. The data processing department grew dramatically and its vice-president, Roy Robinson, brought many newcomers into the company.

Except for professional skills like data processing, the company hired all employees at the store level, promoting only from within. This made for very company-oriented employees, but also meant that the data processing professionals hired from outside could become "outsiders," not able to work and communicate effectively with home-grown managers. Robinson realized that it would be easy for his department to be separate from the rest of Drug Mart.

He recognized that data processing people, although professionals, are sometimes prone to being prima donnas. The field has many people who care first about their profession and second about the company in which they work. They could never make it in Drug Mart with that type of attitude. It was his job to make each one of his people part of the team, one of the "insiders."

Robinson set a climate for success for new employees in his department and got them involved by putting new data processing people through a three-day tour of the company. It was designed especially for them. When they saw the time the firm invested in this, they realized Robinson was serious about being a member of the Drug Mart team. He began by spending a morning with them, showing them why their new place of work was such a great company. Then they visited every facility.

He also told them to speak only English—no computer talk. Data processing was not an end unto itself, just the means to an end. When they were done with the introductory program, they were ready for success at Drug Mart.

## HOW TO IMPROVE YOUR EFFECTIVENESS BY SETTING A CLIMATE FOR SUCCESS

In the crush of doing business, in the interest of doing their best to get their jobs done, managers often begin work on the task in front of them without paying attention to the conditions in which they're trying to work. They're such good soldiers that they go right to the task assigned, unconscious of the climate in which they are trying to attain success.

Suppose you were given a pen lying on the center of a table, and had the job of getting the pen to the floor. If you attacked the job the way most managers normally attack real problems in their work, the first thing you would do would be to start pushing the pen down, in the direction of the floor—a straightforward, no-nonsense, let's-get-down-to-business approach. Of course, the pen isn't going to reach the floor this way unless you break the table.

Judging by the way managers typically do business, what would be the usual next thing to do? Get more people on the job to help push down on the pen. You know, try again and stick to it. If a little didn't work, try more.

If someone came along and suggested that it might be a good idea to push the pen sideways for awhile, what response would be likely? Remember, we're talking about the way you handle real company problems, not just some simplistic analogy. Wouldn't the idea be brushed aside as a waste of time? People would say, "That's not the direction we need to go and we're behind already." In fact, most managers pride themselves on their ability to be able to bring "more resources to bear" on problems.

So if someone came along and suggested that the company might spend some time pushing the pen sideways, you might say it was a waste of time since it doesn't forward the movement of the pen toward the floor. And, of course, it doesn't—yet. But pushing the pen sideways *is* movement toward setting a climate for success in the job of getting the pen to the floor. In fact, knowing about gravity, you know that if you get the pen past the edge of the table, a climate for success will be set that makes the job of getting the pen to the floor an effortless one.

If you set a climate for success, success will ultimately occur. If you work in a climate for failure, failure will ultimately occur, or the cost of the "success" will be so great that it negates the effort and makes it a failure. In the case of the pen, if you have enough force you might be able to collapse the table and get the pen to the floor. But the loss of the table would probably make the venture a failure.

As a manager, it's important that you take the time to set the appropriate climate for success. Often you do it naturally and effectively without even realizing you're doing it. You can improve your effectiveness by becoming more proficient at producing the right environment.

```
┌──────────────── MBI ACTIONS ────────────────┐
│                                               │
│  #25. Pick a project you're about to launch   │
│     with several people. Plan what's needed   │
│     to ensure a climate for success and       │
│     provide it. If you're uncertain, seek     │
│     advice from the people involved on        │
│     what's needed and how it can be achieved. │
│     Watch how the extra time and energy       │
│     spent at first pays off later.            │
│                                               │
└───────────────────────────────────────────────┘
```

## MANAGING THE CLIMATE VS. MANAGING THE DETAILS

Most managers recognize that it's impossible to manage all the details of the organization they lead. Those who don't know this get hopelessly lost in a mire of pettiness, fall behind, and miss major issues. However, many who stay out of minor issues forget their responsibility to create the climate in which all the details are executed. Remember the three facts about the climate? It's obvious that these managers are susceptible to trouble by relying on their unconscious leadership to get the job done.

### Applying Management by Exception

To avoid getting mired in details, effective leaders use management by exception, paying direct attention only to exceptional issues and staying out of matters that fall within predetermined limits. For example, you might decide not to look at absenteeism data if it's less than 6 percent and more than 3 percent. It's not worth your time because it's normal. If it goes to more or less, you'll find out why.

Probably 80 percent of the details you're concerned with fall within normal limits, with 20 percent being reported to you as exceptionally good or bad. Even though you don't have enough time to attend directly to all the normal details of your organization, you must discover how to exert influence over the details you won't personally supervise.

In dealing with the exceptional 20 percent, study the matters to determine what are the factors behind the extraordinary success or failure. Find ways to promote the good. Go to the source of the bad and make corrections for the future. Take care of anything that needs your personal touch.

With the 80 percent of the details that fall within the predetermined limits of normalcy, be sure to manage the climate in which the details are being accomplished. While this may seem overly simple, it is the essence of effective managing. The most neglected responsibility is managing the climate. It's also one of the most creative facets of management.

## How to Use The Question of Influence In Managing the Climate

The effect of the climate on the workplace was seen in one of the earliest and most famous of management studies, done by Elton Mayo in 1927 at the Hawthorne Plant of Western Electric. The investigators suspected that increasing the lighting of the production area would increase productivity. And it proved to be true.

Only the investigators were in for a big surprise, because when they turned the lights lower, productivity increased again. They changed a series of variables only to find that productivity kept increasing, whether they made working conditions better or worse.

Finally, they found that the critical difference didn't come from the specific changes, but from the new feeling of the workers that management cared about them. The experiments had created a new climate, and this climate affected everything in the workplace. Changing the lighting was just one of the details in a larger environmental change, one of caring about employees. This "caring" climate proved to be conducive to more productivity.

The lesson learned: If you alter the climate, the work of

the organization is affected. For many years, managers have recognized that their actions could affect the climate of the workplace, in both positive and negative ways. Good managers take responsibility for their acts.

But the essential experience of leadership, YOU CAN NEVER NOT LEAD, brings us to a more potent understanding. Since there's always a climate, and since you always influence it, you are responsible for it whether you are conscious of it or not. And you affect it not merely by what you do, but also by what you don't do. Looking back at the Hawthorne experiments, we can conclude that, before the investigation, management's failure to display interest in the workers was responsible for lower production. All those years that management had not shown interest and care had led the company to less than maximum productivity and profit.

Apply The Question of Influence to the climate: *What did I do (or not do) to make this climate?* Look not only to your action, but also to your lack of action. If the climate's right, keep it up. If not, it's time for a change in you, and that may mean stepping out of character.

### Don't Look the Other Way—You're Still the Boss

Everyone in America knew that the Big Three automakers used to make bad cars on Mondays and Fridays. There were many explanations. One of the most obvious was the excessive absenteeism on those days, which caused production lines to be operated with too many fill-ins and which, in turn, resulted in low morale and quality.

Management must have recognized this, too. Yet what did they do to change the climate? Apparently nothing much, since it went on for years. They acted as if "this is just the way things are." These were the circumstances in the workplace, the facts of life, beyond their control. Management did its best under the circumstances.

But, in fact, management's lack of decisive action to change the climate was the equivalent of directing the workers to produce poor quality cars on Mondays and Fridays.

Their lack of action was as effective as any campaign to reduce quality on those days could have been. By looking the other way, they were creating the climate.

They could have shut down plants on Mondays and Fridays. That would have gotten some attention and shown they were seriously concerned about quality. Then, if Tuesdays and Thursdays went bad, close down on those days, too. It wouldn't have taken long to get the message across.

Management could have created the appropriate climate for quality and customer care. It's more likely that they didn't sincerely care enough about quality—and that an environment of *Not caring enough* existed in the plants as well. Management's tolerance of a bad situation was taken as approval to perpetuate it.

Management abdicates its responsibility when it does its best under the circumstances without applying full force to altering the circumstances. It means the company is being managed by circumstances, not by the managers.

When you feel you're a victim of circumstances, consider what Ralph Waldo Emerson said: "You think me the child of my circumstances; I make my circumstances."[2]

Circumstances, climate, condition, environment—all words to describe the aggregate of the surroundings which affect the effort being expended. While you may feel that you cannot control many factors outside your company, recognize that you can affect the entire climate within your organization.

Even when you can't find a way to manage the climate, you should learn from the great salesperson: Take the useful point of view. Assume that you make it happen—as Emerson assumed. Do it for two reasons. First, it's the truth. Second, it's the only way to find answers that will help you bring your organization under your control. Ask The Question of Influence: "What did I do (or not do) to make this climate?"

*Self-Check*

How about your control of the climate of your organization? Ask yourself:

*–How often do I stop to notice the climate?*

*–If I feel that the atmosphere is not right, will I take the time to make it right, or just do the best I can under the conditions?*

*–Do I observe myself to see how I affect the climate of my organization?*

---

**— MBI ACTIONS —**

**#26.** Observe an aspect of the climate of your organization that is detrimental. Recognize where and how your tolerance in the past has caused this climate to endure.

**#27.** List the climate conditions associated with your industry, location, seasonality, or economy that you have accepted in the past as permanent, and therefore have not attempted to change. Think of a company in each case which proves to you by their exceptional behavior that they have created their own internal climate despite conventional wisdom.

---

**HOW TO GAIN POTENCY BY MANAGING THE CLIMATE**

Let's look directly at the power of managing the climate. Consider this: You can't draw a straight line on a curved surface. No matter how hard you work, how earnest and sincere you are, you will never get a straight line on a curved surface.

Your organization has conditions that are almost as striking. You can't get effective work out of two interacting departments if the climate between them is bitter and adversarial. Even though you may use your personal force in a given problem situation, operations will return to the normal ineffective way when you leave things alone, unless you alter the climate. It may work in any given instance, and it may work between certain individuals in the two departments, but normal operations will remain ineffective in a climate that is bitter and adversarial.

You can't develop a system that will work effectively between the two departments. No amount of detailed management will overcome it. You can achieve real success only by recognizing the ineffective climate and creating an effective one.

On the other hand, if two departments are working in a climate of respect and cooperation, they will be effective most of the time even with the worst of systems. This doesn't deny the importance of good systems, but emphasizes that the climate is more important than any details, because the climate affects or determines the details.

Many a consultant, while trying to implement some key system, has known the effort was doomed to failure because management didn't set up a climate for success. And many a company has people working with awful systems but still generating success because there's a climate that gets the job done. While it's best to have the right climate and the right systems, if you only have one, make it be the climate. In a good environment, the people will either make the present system work, devise a new system that works better, or tell you to get someone in to develop a new system.

If the climate of your organization is *Protect your turf,* don't expect much open flow of information. You'd do better to work on the climate than to develop new reporting procedures or chase issues down one by one.

If the climate is *Poor attention to details,* don't be surprised that bills are not rendered, credits not taken, orders are lost, inventories are erratic. Don't hunt the details, change the climate.

If the climate is *The boss never comes out here and doesn't care,* you can expect turnover, alienation, self-serving behavior, cutting corners. Don't tighten down procedures, change the climate.

If the climate of your organization is *I know I'm important here and management cares about me,* look for innovation, receptiveness to new ideas, low waste, good attendance. Don't get too lost in promoting individual results; do everything needed to maintain the climate.

If the climate is *We care about the customer,* expect to find courtesy, smiling faces, patience, listening. Don't talk up the individual positive traits as much as acknowledge the prevailing climate.

Whether the situation is bad or good, the details are the natural fallout of the climate in which the work is done. The power you have as a manager is to create the climate. Certainly, you must manage the exceptional details, both good and bad. Encourage the good and find how to stop the bad, correcting those cases that require your direct intervention. And always use your Managing By Influence leverage to influence the climate.

---
### MBI ACTIONS

**#28.** Take a series of related issues that please you and see what climate produces them. Do what you can to acknowledge and reinforce that climate.

**#29.** Take issues that displease you. What climate perpetuates them? Do what you can to alter the climate. Get help from those involved. When you've changed the climate, see how the details fall into place.
---

### Stimulate a Climate That Supports Your Competitive Strategy

Every company has a strategy for competing in the marketplace. Many times these strategies are unconscious and unplanned and result in random, ineffective behavior. But in successful organizations a good strategy exists, whether clearly defined and stated or not. Strategies are customer oriented. All companies also have a climate, even if not recognized. Since climate is company oriented, management must make the company-oriented climate support the customer-oriented strategy.[3]

If quick turnaround of work is the cornerstone of your

service, you'll need a climate which fosters that pace, which creates a willingness to turn away opportunities that don't contribute to your strategy, always looking for ways to do the job faster. This will require a climate different from the one in an organization whose strategy focuses on careful, individualized attention to the customer's particular requirements. The values are different—not wrong, but different.

## HOW MANAGING THE CLIMATE YIELDS DYNAMIC LEVERAGE: A PRESIDENT SAVES HIS COMPANY

A building services company, call it Hennison Maintenance Services Corporation of Cleveland, had a lawn care division that was losing money. Ivan Norbert, president of Hennison, almost dropped the lawn business, but decided to try another year.

The season began with difficulty. That particular spring brought the most rainfall in the area's history, causing many problems. Norbert's vice-president, who managed the division, got deeply discouraged and quit.

The grass grew so quickly that the crews would always find long grass which was hard on the equipment and slow to cut. It was also wet. As a result, there was lots of grass to rake. The crews normally didn't need to rake. Expenses grew and crews were working harder and longer than reasonable on days when it didn't rain. Equipment was breaking down because of the abuse. Workers were quitting because the bad weather caused many days off which meant small paychecks.

Lawn mowers were slipping in the wet grass. A riding mower slid through an apartment window and a hand mower slipped down a hill and crashed into a car. Customers were angry. There was no satisfaction from the work. The equipment maintenance crew was ready to quit because of overwork, and everyone had the feeling that Hennison would fold its lawn division in the middle of the season.

If they had folded, Hennison's customers would have hired other companies to complete the season contracts and would have sued Hennison for the higher costs of bringing in these new crews. The entire company was threatened.

Ivan Norbert decided that if he didn't do something right away they'd be out of business in a very short time. Norbert had none of the specialized knowledge needed for management of lawn care, and his recently promoted manager was getting shaky. He was a drowning man and had to grasp for any straw he could. What could he do? He decided to change everyone's attitude. With that changed, they could limp through the season.

One day, he picked something positive that happened and went into the shop and said very loudly, "We've turned the corner. Everything's going to be all right." The mechanics were amazed to hear him say that. They challenged him, but he backed it up with some facts. The important thing was that he'd said, "We've turned the corner."

Later, he told the same thing to his manager, Chuck. He backed it up with a few facts. At first Chuck was skeptical, but he was willing to consider it. Then Norbert told the office staff. They assumed he knew what he was talking about, except for the complaint calls they were answering. He told them that the complaints were getting smaller and less important and that they would change shortly. Every time something good happened, he said it proved they had turned the corner.

After several days of this, Chuck started to spread the word, too. Each person was telling others and they were believing it. Their actions showed more confidence, and they did a better job since they were more confident. The new climate of confidence and success was taking hold, and the work was being positively affected by it. Workers felt better and stopped quitting; the company started to catch up with its normal schedule.

One day, Chuck had a lot of difficulties. He told Ivan Norbert that Norbert didn't know how bad it was because he wasn't there in the mornings when the crews went out. Norbert said, "What time?" Chuck said, "Seven o'clock."

At 6:30 the next morning, Norbert showed up. He made things work out. Even though he didn't know much about what they were doing, just his presence made the difference. And he kept telling everyone that it was all working out now. "Just keep up the good work." After four days of Norbert's coming in at 6:30, Chuck admitted that it was going better, even in the morning. Everything improved because the people weren't so down on themselves. The detrimental climate had been replaced with one that supported the operation.

Hennison limped through the rest of the lawn care season, which was their last one. They lost some money, but Norbert didn't jeopardize the main business. Hennison had to make several billing adjustments, but there were no lawsuits. Chuck helped sell the equipment and Norbert made a favorable settlement with Chuck to keep him interested until the business could be wrapped up. He then helped Chuck find new work.

Ivan Norbert says, "I believe it was the most *creative* management I've ever done. It was creative in that I started with nothing and created a success. And I did it all by working on the climate. The old environment was killing us. The new one saved us. Of course, I can tell you today that the most *destructive* thing I've ever done in management was to be unaware of the old climate and let it endure. But once I recognized the situation, I didn't wait until things turned around. I *made* them turn around just by managing the climate. And no one knew about my doubts."

But you've done the same. It's just time to be more conscious about it and more practiced at the techniques of creating, monitoring, and managing a climate.

---

## MBI ACTIONS

**#30.** Create a worthwhile climate in your organization starting from scratch. Don't discuss your project with anyone—just do it. Use all your ability to plan and monitor your results. Discover your own power.

## HOW MANAGING THE CLIMATE CREATED A TURNAROUND
## AT UNITED AIRLINES

Ed Carlson took over as chief executive officer of United Airlines in 1970. Times were difficult and revenues were headed down. When he came to United, he observed a bureaucracy which stifled communication, progress, innovation, and every other valuable part of an organization that can get lost in the red tape of a hierarchical, centralized company. Rather than wait to attack these basic issues one at a time, he set out to change the entire climate at United without blocking the parts of the structure that worked.

Recognizing the need to find out what was happening at the working levels and to show genuine interest, he began MBWA: Management By Walking About. He went into the field and observed a climate he called NETMA: Nobody Ever Tells Me Anything. So he began sharing information in the field that had been considered too private. This started to build a climate of trust and involvement.[4]

Naturally, Carlson used many strategies to bring about a shift in United. But how could one man, at the top of an organization of 65,000 people, have maximum effect in the least time? He did it by determining the climate, finding what he wanted to change, and being visible so he could change it. The grapevine spreads information faster than the corporate communication system, and it's more trusted.

Ed Carlson's ability to create a more appropriate climate started with his observation of the existing conditions. No matter how good your intentions and plans, if you don't know where you are at the moment, you're still lost.

For example, suppose you're in a car at an intersection in an unfamiliar city, sitting with a map of the city in your hands. Your destination is marked on the map with a circle. You look up and find that someone has taken the street signs. Even with your goal determined and a detailed set of plans, you still can't get there because you don't know where you are at the moment.

Most managers, most of the time, pay lots of attention to where their organization *has been,* and where they plan it *will be,* without attending to where *it is now.* (Most of us do that in our private lives, too.)

Furthermore, the current management information that does get reviewed is usually very detailed and almost always task oriented rather than organization oriented. That is, the reports measure the amount of task the company does but don't measure the way the company works at it. The information is task oriented to the exclusion of being process oriented.

To be effective in managing your organization, you must be effective in managing the climate. The first step to managing the climate is monitoring it.

## CLIMATE CHECK: A TECHNIQUE FOR MONITORING THE CLIMATE

To enable you to monitor the climate of your organization, use the exercise we call Climate Check. It's a technique for observing the present climate of your company at any given instant. Regular use will also enhance your general awareness of the climate at all times.

### How to Conduct a Climate Check

Climate Check is a snapshot look at the climate of the organization you are monitoring. It can be used for the entire organization, a department, a project, or a person. As a measure of the moment, it isn't comparative, although it may express direction. This is much like the weatherman's report of the barometric pressure: 30.15 inches of mercury and falling. This doesn't compare to any point in the past except to point out that it's in a falling mode at the moment.

You'll find it worthwhile to record and retain your Climate Checks over a period of time. Then you can look back to see trends and recognize progress or deterioration that may have happened so slowly that you failed to notice. But at any given time, the Climate Check freezes your observation of the present.

Climate Check asks: What is the climate of the organization now? You can use other words to help bring responses, such as atmosphere, environment, condition, tone, or context. Respond with adjectives and phrases that describe the climate. Avoid getting involved in the details.

```
┌──────────────── MBI ACTIONS ────────────────┐
│                                              │
│  #31. Describe the climate of your organization as it is │
│     now. Write it using adjectives or short phrases. Do it in │
│     fewer than twenty-five words and in less than five │
│     minutes.                                 │
│                                              │
│  #32. If you like the climate you see, determine how to │
│     sustain that environment. If some part of it is not good │
│     for the company, plan how to change it. Ask· "What did │
│     I do (or not do) to make this climate?" │
│                                              │
└──────────────────────────────────────────────┘
```

**Provocative Words and Phrases to Use in a Climate Check**

These are some words and phrases often used in Climate Check.

| | |
|---|---|
| Adolescent | Mature |
| Busy | Scared |
| Cynical | Scattered |
| Efficient | Slow |
| Exhausted | Sloppy |
| Happy | Tense |
| Harmonious | Tired |
| Inefficient | Trusting |
| Infantile | Wasteful |

A team
Able to count on each other
Cash poor
Coming together

Department mentality, not company mentality

Dollars more important than customers

Each one for him/herself

Enjoy working together but forget we're here to do a job

Five separate operations sharing a building

Focused on quality

Forgetting the customer

Friction between departments

Full of cliques

Good individual strengths, weak on teamwork

Growth oriented

Hoping it will all work out

Internal politics causing confusion in customers

It's our big season

Lack of communication

Losers' attitude

Lost in details

Management vs. labor

Market, market, market

Me first

Nobody listening to workers

Not enough preventive maintenance of the people

Not working to common purpose and goals

Number one in our field

On vacation

One big family

Overstaffed

Over the hill

Profit is a four letter word

Protect your own turf

Pulling together

Taking care of business

Technically up-to-date, production out-of-date

Too busy to take care of ourselves

Too many chiefs

Two companies: old-timers vs. newcomers

Unchallenged

Understaffed

Unsure of goals

Well-oiled machine

Without direction

Working toward common goals

---

## MBI ACTIONS

**#33.** Pick a problem situation. Do a Climate Check.

---

### When to Do a Climate Check

Set a time aside, as Sidney Rittenberg did in solitary confinement, to think quietly about your organization. Do it regularly each week. On Mondays, do Climate Check and make your plans. On Fridays, do Climate Check to see your results. Make a note on your calendar to do it as part of your job. Use Climate Check to start a project and monitor progress. Use it in a problem situation or when you suspect something is out of place but you're not sure what. Once you do Climate Check and gain from it, you won't stop. But you may not get much out of it at first. It takes some practice. Try it for a month before you make a judgement.

### What to Do With the Results

After a Climate Check, ask yourself two questions. First, what parts of the present climate do I want to change and what parts should I keep? Second, ask The Question of Influence to determine what you're doing to produce the present climate, and what you can do to create the new climate you desire or to reinforce the climate you wish to keep.

Then plan your strategy. In many cases, it will be a very short-term issue. Other times, it will require most of your management skills. Pick a strategy consistent with the timeliness, staying power, and resources available. The trick is to attack the climate, not the details.

Now determine the specific tactics you'll use. Sometimes it may be enough just to wait until the right moment to act unfolds. Other times you'll do better to create a situation that gives you a chance to apply your leadership. If you need to sustain a plan for several days or longer, use your daily calendar and other resources such as a secretary to support your implementation. Treat it as an important part of your job, calling for your full creativity and power.

After a reasonable period, take time to gather evidence and do another Climate Check which will either verify that the job is done or point to more effort needed.

---

### MBI ACTIONS

**#34.** Regarding the Climate Check you just did on a problem, ask The Question of Influence. Act to make a new climate and watch for resolution of the problem. If needed, get advice from others.

**#35.** Use Climate Check at the start of a meeting, and invite your colleagues to do it with you. If you find the environment hostile to the goals of your meeting, take the time to work on these circumstances rather than plunge ahead with your meeting. Set up a climate for success.

For example, if you see the climate of a meeting among department heads is one of distrust, there's no point in going on. Get the matter of distrust to the surface. See if the others recognize it. Find out how they feel about working in that climate. Perhaps you can get their assistance to form a new relationship in a new climate.

If you spend your meeting on the issue of distrust, it may not directly resolve your current problem, but it may solve the problem indirectly by changing the environment in which the departments work. And there's probably little chance of solving the original problem in a climate of distrust anyway. All you'd get is finger pointing and protection of turf. In fact, your willingness to address the problem and your statement of desire for change will make a difference. If you don't address it in the meeting, even though it exists, then you're training your people to continue acting that way.

### How to Train Others to Do a Climate Check

It will be worth your while to train others to use Climate Check because it will focus them on the climate, rather than just on the details. If you get your immediate staff doing a Climate Check of your entire organization—not just of their own areas—you'll be teaching them how to take a larger point of view. This will make their work more appropriate to the needs of your whole organization rather than just their own departments.

---

## MBI ACTIONS

**#36.** At a staff meeting or project meeting, have your staff do Climate Check on the entire organization you manage and also on their own departments or functions. Explain the benefits so they'll be willing to attack Climate Check as if it's important, and ask them to withhold judgement of its usefulness until they've done it awhile.

**#37.** If you don't have staff meetings, have a meeting just for the purpose of training your people and getting their ideas. All present should do a Climate Check of the overall organization, of their own areas of the organization, and of themselves. Such an interchange among your people can be a learning experience in and of itself.

If they feel they don't know the climate of the whole organization, only their own areas, ask them to be more aware of it in the future. Tell them you'll keep them better informed. If they're surprised by the climate of other areas, consider holding staff meetings just to do Climate Check so all your people can see how they fit into the whole.

The entire process of engaging your staff in Climate Check will, in itself, create a climate. At the end of the meeting, do a quick Climate Check on the meeting. This process may not end in a new harmony, but it may reveal the issues that separate your people. If so, it's an opportunity for you to use your leadership and confront these issues head on.

Climate Check provides a useful form of "shorthand communication" for any meeting of any number of people. Use it when you're walking through your shop or office. Get your people to the point where they think Climate Check every time they see you. Soon you'll have created a climate in which everyone monitors the climate. This will focus all your people on their own leverage.

## How to Sense the Climate

There are no barometers or thermometers for measuring the climate of your organization. Certain monitoring points can help you sense the atmosphere. Keep your eye on production, costs, delivery times, and other hard indicators of how well you're doing. Add in other factors, such as absenteeism, waste, and customer complaints. Then consider the intangibles, such as pride, attitude, tension, backbiting, and protection of turf.

Obviously, this isn't a precise science, but it works. Your brain is good enough at inductive thinking and analysis to translate all this diverse data into a generalized statement about the climate of your organization.

Beyond that, there's your intuition—your "gut" feeling. If you don't trust your own ability to be intuitive, step out of character, and test it for awhile. Tune in to the feeling, the "vibes," or just your own bodily response to the climate. You'll find you can be more accurate than you would have believed.

If you are uncertain, you can simply seek verification from those around you. Ask them if they sense the same climate you do. If they do, trust it. By the way, you will have exerted your influence just by having them stop to recognize the situation. In many cases, improvement of the climate starts automatically with the recognition of an unwanted climate. When asking others about the existing environment, use The Question of Influence to collect some feedback on your impact. This brings the ball back into your court so you can take any action you see fit.

---

The ultimate test of Climate Check is in its usefulness to your leadership. If it's too vague, it won't reveal any point of application for your Managing By Influence leverage. If it's too detailed it will be overwhelming, giving you no leverage. If it's shallow and insincere it won't give you real information, just fluff. If you can't use your Climate Check, you aren't doing it right yet—keep on practicing.

However, even if it's not being done right, you may still learn something from it. If you find your people are unwilling to get into real matters, you can step back and check the new climate revealed by the misfired Check, recognizing the climate is not safe enough for the truth. Then you can ask The Question of Influence to find out how to change this.

### SEVEN LESSONS IN CLIMATE CHECK

One day Ivan Norbert entered the repair shop at Hennison Maintenance and was struck by the mess on the floor, quite unusual for his crew. As he walked on, no one said hello. He put his antennae out to better gauge the situation. A foreman called in at that moment and the mechanic who answered was very curt on the phone. Something was wrong. He mentally ran a Climate Check: *Angry, short-tempered, unhappy.*

Norbert left the shop, bought a cup of coffee for each of the four mechanics, and returned to announce an impromptu meeting. At first, no one spoke when he asked, "What's new?" The group was tense. He then asked the crew to do Climate Check. They came up with: *No respect from front office, Inconsistent company policies, Edgy, Each man for himself, Can't get work done.*

As the crew stated their observations, the tension eased, everyone feeling better just having acknowledged the situation. Norbert then asked what caused the present climate and if there was anything he did to contribute to it or that he could do to improve it. That opened things up, and the mechanics revealed a disagreement they had had with the payroll people regarding overtime payment. They felt the company had broken its commitment to them. Norbert told them he'd look into it and get it straightened out. He asked, "Can we get rid of this battlefield and return to normal now?" They all had a good laugh.

After talking with the payroll people and resolving the misunderstanding, Norbert went back out to the shop. Thirty minutes had passed, and Norbert was amazed to find the floors swept, the workers chattering as they worked, and the earlier feeling of anger and tension completely dissipated. There was no need to handle each item separately. It was more useful to do Climate Check and take care of all the problems at one time by changing the environment that caused them.

If Norbert had turned around and gone back to his office when he first saw the atmosphere, he would have reinforced it by ignoring it. The crew thanked him for resolving the issue. One man remarked, "In most places, the boss either doesn't notice these things or notices and doesn't care."

---

Lin Grubbs, president of The Jacobs Companies of Landover, MD, had each member of his Executive Committee do Climate Check for the entire company and for his own division.

Ed Dentz, a vice-president, had been responsible only for

the leasing division until he took over management of the truck sales operation in Baltimore three months earlier. As he read his Climate Check, a colleague observed that Dentz had not included anything about the Baltimore operation. Dentz thought for a moment, shook his head, and said, "Thanks for noticing that. It may be just a slip, but it shows me I haven't taken hold there the way I should. Next week will be different."

No doubt Ed Dentz would have gotten involved soon enough, but here a simple observation during Climate Check may have saved the company several weeks without leadership in Baltimore. It's a chance to stand back and take an objective look at the way you work.

———

Dave Lerman, president of Steel Warehouse Company, Inc, a steel service center in South Bend, IN, was doing Climate Check one Monday morning (a regular part of his schedule), when he realized he didn't know the present climate in the plant. If he felt out of touch with his people, they probably felt out of touch with him.

He made a note to walk through the plant that afternoon. As workers called out, "Hi, stranger," he knew he had been away too long. But he hadn't noticed it until he took quiet time to think about his leadership role.

———

Lerman recognized that waste had been unusually high one month. After checking with several people, he found that waste control wasn't on many minds at the moment. He started a one-day campaign to correct this unwanted climate.

He asked everyone he saw that day what his or her department's waste figure was the previous month. He wasn't surprised when nobody knew. He told each person to find out and send him the figure on a note by the end of the day. Then he toured the plant with the plant superintendent and the foreman of each department to ask for a plan to reduce waste in some way. He asked each foreman to monitor next month's waste, compare it to this month's, and send him a report.

By the end of the day, the whole company was buzzing with discussions about waste and Lerman's concern over it. Dave Lerman put a message on his calendar to check for each foreman's report the next month. He took all the notes people had sent him that day with the waste figures and wrote "Thank you, Dave," on each, returning the notes to the senders. Lerman felt satisfied that his staff's temporary neglect of the importance of waste control had been turned around. But he liked the impact so much that he decided to do it again the following month. He was using Managing By Influence leverage.

_____

The Management Board of Valley Lighting of Towson, MD, was doing Climate Check. As each manager revealed the climate of his or her own part of the company, it occurred to Vivian Portnoy, a vice-president, that she had no firsthand experience of the warehouse operation, which was in another building. On further thought, she realized that the top managers seldom stopped in at the warehouse.

Looking back at warehouse manager Ray Jones's report on the warehouse, she could see that they had really neglected this part of Valley Lighting's operation. She made a plan to stop in, and to get other managers to visit more often. As the warehouse personnel received more attention, relations with the main office improved. This situation had existed for years, but Climate Check brought it to Portnoy's awareness so she could act on it.

_____

Dr. Mort Ehudin, a dentist in Fort Washington, MD, has his staff do Climate Check at the weekly staff meeting. When he began this procedure, several people said they couldn't do it because they didn't know about the whole practice, only their own part. Ehudin recognized the truth of this, realizing it explained why the people couldn't cooperate more with each other, even though they seemed to want to.

Starting then, Mort Ehudin had a different person explain her job each week, telling her difficulties and then stating the climate from her point of view. When all were done, they understood each other better and could work in harmony. They continue to do Climate Check each week, and keep each other up-to-date on a daily basis. Everytime someone can't do Climate Check at the staff meeting, she knows she's been out of contact during the week.

———

At The Rouse Company, Bruce Alexander sometimes observes in his division a destructive climate which he refers to as *Division and corporate politics*. As he explained, "This is when people are very concerned about what's happening to other people; gossip, rumors, and backbiting result. The Rouse Company has the least of this I've ever seen or experienced in a company, so it's easy to isolate this problem and deal with it."

When he sees it, he'll tell the person involved, "That's not the way this company operates. Competitiveness and zero-sum games hurt the company, and I won't tolerate it. As good as you are, as much as you do your job, it's so destructive to the environment that is critical to our success, that I just can't allow this to happen. Therefore, you've got to change or leave."

Alexander says, "I think there's a real difference between being sensitive to people and indulging people. And I think those two things are sometimes confused. I don't think it's to anybody's benefit to indulge people in activities that are harmful to the good of the mission. And that's the kind of challenging I've been able to do. People are up to that challenge; they just aren't usually confronted with it.

"Since you're always affecting your people, you need to make it very clear that you don't just talk about principles, you also act on them. People have a feeling for whether integrity really exists or not. All the talking in the world doesn't mean much. You need to make real integrity a high priority by your actions. And every action counts."

You only need to visit the Commercial Development Division of The Rouse Company once to experience the climate of integrity that Bruce Alexander has created using his influence.

## SIXTEEN DO'S AND DON'TS
## OF CLIMATE CHECK

<u>Do</u> Climate Check regularly.

<u>Do</u> Climate Check in writing and retain.

<u>Do</u> Climate Check in twenty-five words or less.

<u>Do</u> Climate Check in five minutes or less.

<u>Do</u> Climate Check with adjectives and short phrases.

<u>Do</u> Climate Check with other people to compare viewpoints.

<u>Do</u> Climate Check at the start of meetings and projects.

<u>Do</u> Climate Check as a means of shorthand communication.

<u>Do</u> Climate Check when you think you have a problem but can't put your finger on it.

<u>Do</u> Climate Check when you come into a new situation.

---

<u>Don't</u> make Climate Check a list of details.

<u>Don't</u> write Climate Check in sentences and prose.

<u>Don't</u> make Climate Check so vague that you can't use it.

<u>Don't</u> review old Climate Checks before you begin.

<u>Don't</u> fill Climate Check with comparative words like better, worse.

<u>Don't</u> make Climate Check a lecture on how things should be; point out how things are.

## THREE FACTS ABOUT THE CLIMATE:
1. There is *always* a climate.
2. The climate *always* affects everyone.
3. You *always* affect the climate.

**This is your Managing By Influence leverage.**

# 5

## How to Create and Implement Climate Strategies

Successful strategies for creating a climate start with realizing the effect of your actions on the climate. Many managers recognize their impact on a specific situation without observing the effect that a specific action has on the climate. While the management of each instance is important, it is the resultant climate that becomes the key indicator of company success.

CEO Izzy Cohen refers to every co-worker at Giant Food as his associate, focusing on the relationship the worker has with the company rather than focusing on the job the worker performs. To Cohen, the relationship with Giant is paramount and everything else stems from that association.

If a man retires after thirty years, whether as porter or manager, Giant has a luncheon in the main office cafeteria. Cohen honors the person for his time and association with the company, not for the particular job he did. Says Cohen, "We wouldn't say this gentleman was a porter, we'd say he stayed in store number 'X' for thirty years. We're careful to give everyone dignity and pride for what they've done in association."

Cohen and Giant Food recognize that every little management action accomplishes two things. First, it makes the given instance work. But, second and more important, it affects the climate. Eventually, the climate affects everything.

Every time Cohen has the opportunity, he uses the term associate or staffer, not employee. He really means it. And the climate is built and maintained in these little steps. Then people go out and work at Giant as if it's their company. And it is!

Al Dobbin says, "I work very diligently at being Al Dobbin, not at being senior vice-president for Operations. I don't feel like a senior vice-president. I feel like a Giant associate. These are my friends, these are people I work with to achieve something for myself as well as for them. I make it very clear that they're important to me. We're working together to achieve something that's good for both of us. And I don't think they look at it as corny. When we go into a store, it's 'Hi, Al. How are you?' And if they're real old-timers, it's probably 'Hi, Dobby.' We're all friends." Every time a newcomer hears an old-timer talk like this, the new person is affected by it. A climate is often built by little things.

## TWELVE TESTED STRATEGIES YOU CAN USE IN YOUR ORGANIZATION

As you read these twelve strategies, look for those that fit your style and temperament. But don't throw away the possibility of stepping out of character and trying one that you might not have used in the past.

Some take lots of time to develop, and some take money. Others are quick and easy. Choose what's appropriate for the climate you wish to change or create. Consider the staying power of the effect, since the faster ones usually won't last as long.

If you start something, resolve to finish it. Otherwise you'll create an overriding climate of false starts and lip service which will undo any good you attain in the short run. If this type of follow-up has not been your typical behavior in the past, step out of character and build a system of self-management that supports you in doing your best for the good of the company.

## 1. Campaigns

A campaign is a connected series of operations designed to bring about a particular result, in this case a climate. Suppose you wanted to produce the climate, *We care about quality*. Of course, you can send out memos and make some speeches, but let's look at other means which may be more effective. Pick the ones that work for you. Use them in combination.

Arrange for the collection of data on rejections, returns, or complaints, whichever is applicable to your business. Have this information sent to you each day. Make the results known through whatever channels of communication you have—bulletin boards, a newsletter, or a note included with paychecks.

Start a committee on quality made up of different organizational levels and departments, cutting across all barriers. Seek ideas, have people take on projects, get the message out to the rest of the company.

Personally take one quality defect a week and trace it to its source, looking for the most basic reason for its occurrence. Publicize the result and ask all other departments to learn from the solution. Keep letting people know that you're serious about the quality issue.

As an area turns around, publicize the new data. Have an interdepartmental meeting to see what others can learn from the success.

Take a company-wide survey with each person rating the quality of the work in his or her own area and in the company as a whole. Ask for one idea per person on how each one can improve the quality of the present work. Conduct the survey periodically, acknowledging progress—or the lack of it. If the survey shows that workers have a higher opinion of the quality than the data supports, you need to educate better.

As you take all these actions, watch for the start of the new climate, *We care about quality*. As soon as you see its beginning, point it out. Promote the new climate. Remember, the specifics of your campaign were designed to create this new atmosphere. Don't dwell on the individual results as much as promote the new climate. Once the climate is firmly in place and acknowledged by everyone, the climate will get the job done.

Now you need to maintain it. Whereas your original campaign focused on individual instances of quality, you can now focus on the climate, *We care about quality*. At your meetings, ask for evidence of this new climate. Use a survey to rate the climate. Ask people to produce proof the new climate exists. Have present workers suggest how to instill it in new workers.

———

A sales organization can launch a campaign called *"Ask-For-A-Referral Week."* By promoting it fully, this climate permeates every aspect of life that week. Salespeople start checking on each other. It buzzes through their heads on sales calls. They talk about it at every meeting. As soon as you say hello, they tell you about the referrals they've asked for. Don't try to sustain it too long. End it before it becomes tiring and boring, but acknowledge the success and get others to acknowledge it as well. Then make a note to check weekly for residual effects. When the time is right, launch the campaign again.

———

How about *"Smile Day?"* The entire staff and all the attorneys in a law firm smiled for one day and changed their behavior forever. For one day, they made sure that every client was smiled at by every person the client came in contact with. The response from clients and the good feeling among staff was so strong that it became a permanent part of the office culture.

———

How effective can a campaign be? Izzy Cohen will walk into a store and the parcel pickup worker, maybe eighteen years old, will come up and say, "Hi, Izzy. How're you doing?" Some people might gasp at this—Cohen is the CEO of a two billion dollar corporation. But Izzy Cohen loves it. These are his associates. He asks a lot from them, and they ask a lot from him. If someone calls him Mr. Cohen, he says, "My name is Izzy." All he wants to do is pay tribute to the truth: At Giant Food everyone's a business associate who needs everyone else. This campaign is endless and crucial for Cohen, who with his associates has created extraordinary success.

### 2. Talking Loudly in the Hallway

The president of an electronics manufacturing company in Los Angeles, call him Tom Wilson, was waiting for an elevator with a member of the Board of Directors. A group of junior level managers who had just finished a class in the training department were waiting, too.

Wilson said to the board member in a voice loud enough to be heard by all, "The best long term investment we can make is in our management. This training costs us money, but it will pay off in the future. Junior level management is the strength of the company."

Wilson could have made that same comment in the training session the junior managers just attended. In fact, he does attend introductory seminars and many other training sessions. But those remarks are heard in a different context than the remarks made between the president and a board member, overheard by the others.

Look at human nature. If someone tells you in private that they admire you, that's nice but you may question their motives. If they tell you in front of someone else, that's more believable. Now, if you overhear that person tell another about how he admires you and you aren't even in sight, so you overhear by accident, then you really believe it. So talking loudly in the hallway has a different impact than talking directly.

And if you call down the hall to someone, "Remember, if we can't get the quality right, don't accept the order—quality is our first priority," everyone hears it. It gets in the air and affects everyone. It enhances your leverage and starts to affect the climate.

———

One manager watches her people and when she sees the climate turn gray and gloomy, she goes to the water cooler at the other side of the office and whistles a light tune as she goes. No one can be gloomy around a whistler. On the way back, she looks for someone at the other end of the hall so she can call out, "Great day, isn't it?" By the time she gets back to her office, things have lightened up.

Another boss likes to walk the halls with his department managers. As they walk, often with the boss's hand on the department manager's arm, the boss congratulates the manager for good work. Using a voice that can be overheard, he acknowledges the workers by telling the department manager how much the boss appreciates their work. The boss often comments, "These people are as good as you keep telling me they are." The whole conversation is only between the boss and the department manager, but it's overheard by many.

If the boss has a concern which he has already discussed privately with the manager, he may express it as they walk. He might say, "I'm afraid we're not as responsive to customers as we should be." He's always conscious of the effect on the climate of his walk, his hand on the manager's arm, and his conversation.

This does not mean being insincere or phony. This can't be just lip service. If it is, you'll be creating a different climate than you intended, one of cynicism and self-service.

———

Talking loudly in the hallway is not a new way of creating a climate. You're already talking in the hallway without even knowing it. Sometimes you say things that create a climate you don't want. Sometimes, just your appearance and the way you walk down the hall give out messages. You always have influence. There are many times you are "in the hallway" each day. Start observing the way you now affect the climate by asking The Question of Influence.

Talking loudly in the hallway offers a low cost, easy way to influence the climate. It can have instant impact, at least for short duration and sometimes for a long term. You don't need to put time aside to do it. It does help to put yourself into a situation where you can get a message across to the right people. But you should always be on the lookout for the chances that already exist. If it looks shallow to you, examine your motives. If you think some things don't need to be said, try saying them anyway. If you never go too far, you're probably not going far enough. If it seems too much like showmanship, remember that, as boss, you're always on stage. If you don't say things, people read their own meaning into your silence.

```
┌─────────────── MBI ACTIONS ───────────────┐
│                                             │
│ #38. Communicate your message, create a     │
│    climate, through the fast, no-cost        │
│    technique of talking loudly in            │
│    the hallway—even if you have to step out  │
│    of character to do it.                    │
│                                             │
└─────────────────────────────────────────────┘
```

### 3. Bulletin Boards

Obviously, a bulletin board is a place to disseminate information. Not so obviously, it also *reflects* the climate of the company. And even less obviously, it can *create* the climate of the organization.

Start observing company bulletin boards at your own company and when you visit others. Sense the climate just from the bulletin boards. Some are faded, yellowed and out of date, with information required by the government and insurance carriers. The information consists of formal mutterings from the top of the hierarchy down to the workers. Check another and you see some signs of the community of the organization. There are notices for teams and picnics. Perhaps a few cartoons have been put up by anonymous contributors, adding to the fun of the organization. This board reflects a different climate. A different bulletin board might tell of open company meetings to discuss company problems or issues. Perhaps there are notices of quality circle meetings. The board may carry an award issued to a worker or department.

Reading the company bulletin boards can help you monitor the climate of the organization. In fact, you might add this to your own Climate Check. Now let's get more creative. How do you manage an organization using a bulletin board?

Consider the type of information you share with your organization. For instance, what would you be saying if you put up company production, shipment, and quality records on the bulletin board in all departments? You'd be telling people that you feel they're important and interested enough in *our* company to care about this. And that you trust them enough to share information that normally isn't made known to outsiders. This type of information on the bulletin board creates a climate of, *This is our company—All of ours.*

By posting information in every department which tells of the performance of all the other departments, you promote the climate, *We're all one company. The wins and losses of each department are the wins and losses of all of us.* (They are, aren't they?) You encourage interdepartmental conversation about problems. If you receive a letter of acknowledgment from a customer, either good or bad, put it on the board. If the letter shows that someone was a star, add your own comments to give credit where due. If there's a problem to be solved, comment on how the company is working to overcome the difficulty. You might ask for suggestions. You never know where an answer will come from. The important thing is to involve everyone in these intracompany issues and create the climate, *This is our company—All of ours.* Use everything you can.

If a department does a great job, write a letter to the manager and put a copy on the bulletin board. Let everyone see a climate of acknowledgment. Add a note to the bulletin board copy encouraging people to congratulate the department on their own. After you discover that people have thanked the department as you asked them to, put a "thank you" note on the board acknowledging them for helping you do your job.

Make the bulletin board an active part of management. Ask for feedback on the board. Announce campaigns, like "Smile Day." Try "Thank a Co-Worker Day." Make the bulletin board a place that people check out regularly because they don't want to miss what's happening.

Recognize the effect these actions have on the climate. If you get the climate right, the rest will fall into place. The bulletin board is more than a place to disseminate information. It's a place to create the organization's climate using little things that can be accomplished with little expense. Once it gets going, it can be a vital part of your company's culture and communication system.

The quality, type, and timeliness of the information on the board reflect the relationship you share with the people you lead. See how you've used your bulletin boards to create the present climate. Ask The Question of Influence.

## 4. Meetings

All managers use meetings to solve problems, plan, control, and exchange information. Look beyond these obvious uses of meetings to consider climate strategies.

Generally, problem-solving meetings are attended by people within the department(s) affected and by people from the same approximate level of organization. See what happens when you invite people from outside the directly affected area(s) and people from several levels, including workers. First, it becomes a "company problem" rather than a "department problem." Now everybody's involved in the need to find and implement a solution. And the worker's point of view is represented so it's easier to implement. The workers get in on information they seldom hear about, so it builds a climate of trust between workers and managers. This helps on all issues, not just this particular problem. If you have a very friendly customer, you might invite him or her to a meeting to get that point of view represented. If not, let someone from the sales department sit in.

While it might be threatening at first, if you do it right and set up a climate of trust by talking with the parties beforehand, you can take a big bite out of a bad climate called *Protect your turf.*

You set a climate of mutual involvement and concern by inviting all these people and disclosing all this information. The informal communication that emanates from these meetings can broadcast a message that it would be impossible to deliver any other way. Naturally, it can't be contrived or false, or it won't work.

The very act of acknowledging and confronting the existence of a problem can create the climate of solution. If all parties agree that a problem exists and that they all want to solve it, they can go back to their own departments and pass the word to their workers that *We're all in this together*—not, *It's us against them.*

---

Now consider a different kind of meeting. Most meetings are held to discuss a given situation or to monitor the task. Seldom do people meet to monitor the process, that is, the way we do the work and how we are working together. Little time is spent planning, monitoring, and creating the climate of the organization itself.

---

## MBI ACTIONS

**#39.** Hold meetings with different mixes of managers and workers to discuss the climate of the organization. Have each person do Climate Check. Then ask each one how the company can maintain the desirable aspects of the climate. On those aspects that aren't desirable or satisfactory, ask how they feel the company could improve the climate. Then ask each of them what

> he or she would be willing to do personally to enhance the climate.
>
> Create an atmosphere of concern for the climate—with everyone taking individual responsibility for it. The very act of inviting them and asking them will start the process. Determine how you can extend your influence by having everyone focused on the best climate.

## 5. Posters

China was managed for years with posters. Mao Tse-tung ran a cultural revolution with them. These posters did more than just get some information out to the people. They set the entire cultural climate of a nation.

Safety and security have been promoted with posters for years. The idea is to create a safety- or security-oriented climate, affecting every worker and all that they do. And it has been found to work. Now quality is being promoted this same way.

Use these lessons to promote whatever climate you plan. Advertising experts will tell you that repetition of messages works. Combine posters with other methods to create the atmosphere. If your budget is big, have posters done professionally. If money is an issue—if your organization is small—make a poster from other pictures or posters. Use inexpensive means of duplication. The quality of the poster is secondary to its relevance.

What climate can you promote? Any one you want, for example: *Details count; The customer pays our wages; Every problem is a company problem; You're either part of the solution or part of the problem; Give a damn, it's your company.*

## 6. Newsletters

In-house newsletters can be expensive and take lots of time or they can be low in cost and easy to do. Your newsletter may be photocopied and put in with paychecks (and put on the bulletin board also, of course) or it may be printed with art work and mailed to the employees' homes. It's nice to mail the newsletters so your message reaches those people who support your workers.

While the newsletter is informative, the Managing By Influence leverage comes from the climate it promotes. To begin with, its very existence shows your concern for communication. Most CEOs will use the house publication to send a written message. Consider the other messages that can be delivered. Why not include information that makes the reader feel like an insider? Include important facts about production, schedules, waste levels, absenteeism, reject rates and other information you would share with your partners. If you can treat the workers similar to the way you treat your managers, you can create a climate that makes managers of them all. That's part of the success Japan has had—evoking a sense of responsibility in people that makes them self-managed.

Get editorial advice from people who represent the readers. Ask them how to promote a sense of belonging and knowledge among the readers. Be sure that the newsletter is timely and fits in with other climate strategies in the company.

## 7. The Grapevine

Every company has its grapevine. In many cases it's a rumor or gossip mill. In the best cases, though, it's a useful way of getting the word around quickly and informally. Says Al Dobbin, "We're blessed at Giant because we have a formal structure but we're an informal company." It starts with CEO Izzy Cohen, who relates, "I answer my own phone, and there isn't anybody who can't call me, and there isn't anybody who can't come into my office."

Rumors and gossip are unhealthy for a company. They are carried on for personal benefit, not for the good of the company. They can cause personal harm and much misinformation. But good informal communication can be very much in the company's interest and in the interest of all the workers.

Plant your message into the grapevine. Pass out well-founded information. Create an environment by making input at several places so the message will crisscross and reinforce itself. This is a great advantage of the grapevine. It makes mountains out of molehills. Make a mountain out of the company's desire to have workers involved in problem solution, in quality control, in customer satisfaction. You can be sure that the grapevine is already tuned in to you, so make the most of an opportunity.

---

## MBI ACTIONS

**#40.** Put a message into the grapevine at five different points. See how long it takes to come back to you, and notice how it affects the climate. This is a no-cost method that really works.

---

Izzy Cohen has a more formal way to promote informal communication, a program called "Letters to Izzy." Cohen says, "Anyone can write, and we average ten letters per month. It's confidential and the individual gets a direct answer. So they feel the door's open, and it is."

Along the same lines, Al Dobbin heads a program called "Lunch With Dobbin." He explains, "I invite people from our stores to lunch. I send out invitations. We get swamped with requests and we randomly select twenty to thirty people to come to lunch. From department managers on down, we have union people, cashiers, porters—everybody. We sit down and have lunch together and then talk about Giant."

Dobbin continues, "But 'Lunch With Dobbin' is not a personal grievance session. If they have a complaint, there's a procedure to deal with their individual problem. I want them to tell me what we can do to make Giant a better company, and what we can do overall to make it a better place to work. We take these suggestions and use them if we can. It gives everyone a chance to deal one-on-one with me and for me to deal one-on-one with them, which has gotten difficult for me to do, with 144 stores and almost 20,000 people." Each associate leaves to take a message back to the stores, keeping the informal communication alive with company-oriented news.

## 8. Walking About

The term Management By Walking About (MBWA) was made famous by Ed Carlson of United Airlines. But lots of other managers have done it as well. Its power lies in the ability to monitor and influence the climate of the organization, not in the ability to go out and solve individual problems.

It's easy to forget how much can be accomplished by getting out among all the people—managers and workers alike. Even bosses of small offices often get locked into their direct duties and forget to look up from their desks. And in larger organizations, it's particularly easy to lose contact with the people doing the work. There are ways to get around this. If your company has several locations, you can have your regular staff meetings in a different facility each time. Get everyone out to tour the facility. Rather than call field managers into your offices, visit them.

When you come to work, take a different path each day. Take a break and have coffee in the employees' lounge. Talk with people. Share your enthusiasm—all eyes are on you. Prepare yourself so you can acknowledge a department for their success and talk about how good you feel about other departments' successes. Give people current company news; make them feel like insiders. If it's your style, introduce yourself by first name and encourage informality.

Walk with your managers, showing people the warmth and positive regard you have for these managers. Build your managers' images in the workers' eyes. Have your managers introduce you to people you don't know, telling you about them so you can acknowledge them. Your presence alone will have an impact. It's important to people that you have made them a priority. They understand the demands on your time. If you don't walk about, that means something, too. It tells of your priorities, but the message is a different one.

Dave Lerman of Steel Warehouse likes to take visitors on a plant tour. Not only is he proud to show the plant, but it gives him a chance to talk with workers informally and to let them show their family spirit in front of "company." If no visitors are around, he likes to grab someone from the office, taking the opportunity to build greater understanding between the office and plant. When he completes a tour, he feels more in touch with the values the company provides. And his people know the "big boss" cares. It doesn't take long. In fact, it's a nice change of pace.

---

### MBI ACTIONS

**#41.** Take on a one-month project of "Walking About" to create the climate. Here's a word of caution, though. Don't leave walking about to chance or you'll never do it. Make it a scheduled event. Put it on your calendar and give it top priority. Follow it up with letters for the bulletin board or any other special programs you have developed. Get your message into the grapevine.

---

### 9. Quality Circles

A few years ago, when quality circles were thought to be the answer to every problem, many people jumped in and were disappointed. One prominent reason for this unfulfilled expectation: management didn't make the circles a high enough priority and didn't give them the planning, effort and sustained enthusiasm they require.

A second letdown came when management didn't see hard results equal to the hype that introduced quality circles. In this regard, management should consider the soft results that accrue, basically from the effect circles have on the company's climate.

A quality circle program assumes an interest and commitment to the company that is shared by managers and workers alike. Such a program exists in and contributes to a climate of trust. The program permits workers to make a voluntary statement acknowledging their care and concern for the source of their mutual well-being: the company.

The circles often cross lines of responsibility and add to a climate of *One company, with each person responsible for it all.* And the program encourages people to learn about other areas and to seek help from other workers whom they might never ask for help in the normal course of business. The program encourages crossing all lines, including management. This promotes healthier informal communication. Many times, the "stars" come from below. That may seem threatening to middle management, but this only spotlights the need to create a climate of security and company-oriented behavior throughout. Very often middle management is the wellspring of the "protect your turf" attitude.

A quality circle program shows management where it is falling short, particularly in the areas of generating sustained enthusiasm and creating useful new problems such as how to advance the company, instead of reacting to old problems like fixing what doesn't work. The program forces management to plan ahead, not only in product but also in process; not only in holding ground but in upgrading. Since the program's focus is most often on process, it creates a climate that is more process conscious.

Rather than look at a quality circle program as a crisis or a pain in the managerial neck, consider it an opportunity for top management to interact in a potent way, using leverage by managing the climate of the business—even if your whole company is so small that it forms only one circle. A quality circle program also creates a climate of challenge for management to lead the company.

## 10. Reporting Systems

Most reporting systems in companies are task and production oriented. They send information one way (up), discuss the past, focus on reacting to problems, and do little to help the person making the report. Their major contribution to the climate is: "Keep on your toes, play it close to your vest; look good."

Try this reporting system for its positive effect on the climate.

1. Once a week, the lowest level workers report to their managers, answering these questions:
   a. What were my production figures? (Use whatever numbers you monitor, including quality, schedule, customer satisfaction.)
   b. What were my goals?
   c. Last week, what three positive contributions did I make to the company's success that I can acknowledge myself for?
   d. What are the three highest-priority potential problems I face this week? What plan do I have to overcome them?
   e. What one thing am I doing to upgrade my work this week?

2. Each worker discusses this with his or her manager, and they determine how to help each other in these areas during the week. The manager can acknowledge the worker for progress from the prior week. They collaborate on priorities.

3. Each manager then gives the same report to his or her manager, and it keeps rolling up the structure, to the head of the organization.

4. Each manager, starting at the top, also gives the report to his or her people going down the structure. At the end of this process, everyone knows the problems and plans and accomplishments of the people one level up and one level down.

You can put your own touches to it, but this is the basic reporting system to use in order to create valuable climates as well as to manage high priority exceptional details. This system will create an awareness of collaboration across levels, understanding and visibility both up and down, thinking ahead, clear priorities, acknowledgment, upgrading (not just reacting), process consciousness, common interest and commitment to the organization, and respect—all of which will become an important part of the climate of your organization.

On a spot basis, you might try adding questions to regular production-oriented reports or sending out a request for a special report. For example:

1. What did I do to forward quality today?
2. How did I contribute to the reduction of waste today?
3. What is my highest priority tomorrow?
4. In what one way did I advance office security today?
5. How did I reach out to cooperate with a co-worker today?
6. What is my boss's biggest problem tomorrow?
7. How did I help a customer today?
8. How did I thank a co-worker today?

Do these ideas take time? Of course they do. But they're worth every minute of it. The bigger your organization, the more energy it takes from you—but the more you need systems to reach beyond your personal ability to touch people. The discipline will do you good, too. The greatest influence you can have is to affect the climate.

## 11. Insignia

In days gone by, everyone knew the magic of certain insignia. When athletes put on uniforms, they were able to step out of character and do remarkable things for the good of the team. Remember the New York Yankee "pin-stripe" uniforms? And how about putting on the Boston Celtic "green"? Uniforms have always helped create a climate of success and teamwork. Insignia in companies can run from a lapel pin to an identification badge to uniforms.

Everyone at Mort Ehudin's dental practice wears a uniform, including Ehudin. On any day you'll find them all wearing matching shirts and/or sweaters with their names on them. What does it do for them? It creates a climate that reminds them they're all in this together. It tells patients they're being treated by a team. It shows the doctor's trusting relationship with the staff. And, somehow, when they put their uniforms on, they are able to put away any personal pettiness or problems and step out of character for the good of the practice. It's fun to feel that way; it's an important reward of the job—to feel that you belong.

---

As a recognition to the employees of Steel Warehouse, Dave Lerman gave company caps to everyone. The employees loved it. Even the "tough guys" got into the excitement. Now Steel Warehouse gives a company jacket to employees who have been with the company five years. The jackets are very much sought after. People do care and are willing to show it. Notice how it affects the climate.

---

Walk into Al Dobbin's office at Giant's headquarters and you'll see him wearing his company nametag and a button proclaiming the latest promotion in the stores. All the store employees are wearing them and Dobbin is part of the action, even when he's at headquarters. He helps create a climate of *Team* by wearing this much of a uniform. It's all part of the family climate Giant promotes.

## 12. A Purpose and Super-Ordinate Goals

Efforts without purpose are meaningless and isolated. But, with purpose, all work falls into context, can be understood, and becomes satisfying. Every organization has a purpose although it may not be recognized or stated. Write a statement of your company's purpose. See how the workers relate to it. Consider telling the purpose to your customers.

By the way, "to make a profit" is not a valid purpose in

itself. If your *entire* purpose is to make a profit, you're in the wrong business: you should be dealing in illegal drugs. Profit belongs as part of your purpose since profit is needed to sustain the organization. Even your customers want you to make a fair profit. But profit is not the sole purpose for doing business. When it is, businesses fail. Even the most profit-driven entrepreneur recognizes the need to give value, take care of customers, and build a reputation.

If everyone can understand and support the purpose of the organization, they will be able to make decisions and plans based on the purpose. Equally important, they will be able to relate to and support each other in the common context.

As a further refinement of your purpose, you may develop a super-ordinate goal. Pascale and Athos discuss this in *The Art of Japanese Management*.[1] A super-ordinate goal is one which is above all others (as opposed to a sub-ordinate goal which is secondary to others). A super-ordinate goal may focus on the overall company, such as the creation of a family feeling. It may stress the company's position in the marketplace, such as to always be a leader in technology or variety or service. It may give preference to internal issues such as the care of employees, the opportunity to advance, the value of the human being. The super-ordinate goal doesn't exclude other goals, but rather it gives an overriding context to all the organization does. It creates a climate which is unifying and transcends differences.

The purpose and/or super-ordinate goal is also a vital factor when making corporate decisions, determining future plans, resolving conflict or putting a big win or loss into perspective.

---

When Al Hackl founded Colortone Press in Washington, DC, in 1946, he looked to the market to determine the major customer complaints about printers. The answer: work comes out wrong and late. He opened Colortone with an overriding commitment to doing the job right the first time and getting it out on schedule. The company's motto and super-ordinate goal is "Right On Time—Always." Anytime Colortone employees wonder about priorities they need only look to this statement. It's the major criterion in all decisions. Everyone puts it first, starting with Hackl.

## REALIZE THAT ACTIONS SPEAK LOUDER THAN WORDS (AND SO DOES LIP SERVICE)

All these climate strategies require a commitment from management. These are not just smart things to say, words that can build a facade for management. No matter what you say, most people still take the Missouri attitude: "Show me."

When people ask Izzy Cohen what makes Giant successful, he says, "There are three reasons: people, people, people." Those are nice words, but Giant's CEO backs them up. He says, "We don't have lip service. What you see is what you get, and what we say is what we do. There are no magic formulas, no secret recipes in our business. It's attention to basics, and we try to instill the Golden Rule in everyone—you treat everyone the way you'd like to be treated. Like any other business, there's no instant success and no instant failure."

Actions from management must be true to the climate you wish to promote. If Al Hackl sits in a meeting saying, "Cut the costs, it's okay if this job runs late," not only does he cut the bottom out of the main company objective, he also breeds a distrust for management's word and commitment. That's worse than never stating the super-ordinate goal in the first place.

As with Dr. Dave Levine in Chapter 1, your influence can undermine your planned strategies. In fact, your own adherence to the strategy and climate plays a major role in creating and maintaining the atmosphere you want. There are many opportunities to promote your climate. If you let them pass, you make a statement about the priority you really give the climate. If it's not worth your time, energy, effort, or attention, why should the others heed it?

Izzy Cohen tells more of his role at Giant. "From time to time we have meetings with all our managers. I participate in all these meetings, and I cover philosophy and concept while all the other people who are involved in those meetings deal with specifics. I usually wrap up the meetings. We have a yearly presidential award banquet, where I talk about what Giant is. We don't just give lip service when we say something; we mean it and we follow through."

Al Dobbin considers the priorities of his time. "Today, I spend less and less time on managing the task. I spend more time trying to attend to our human resources and other motivational matters. Currently I use 30 percent of my time managing the task and 70 percent managing the management and the way we work together."

Be certain that your actions are consistent with your words. To be sure, occasionally ask yourself The Question of Influence, and use the people around you to monitor your own actions.

## CLIMATE STRATEGIES FROM SEVEN SUCCESSFUL COMPANIES

To enhance your ability to apply these strategies, consider seven successful means of managing the climate of a company. From Thomas Watson Sr.'s management of IBM's formative years to Lee Iacocca's promotion of Chrysler's self-confidence, these case studies are presented to show the potency of influence on the climate.

While the stories may be familiar in terms of their content, think about them in the context of Managing By Influence. Watch how one person can use Managing By Influence leverage without being immersed in every issue.

### Hughes Aircraft: Quality Circles Influence the Climate

They begin and end with management. For quality circles to succeed in a company, management must take an active interest and initiative. In companies where quality circles have not been successful, the blame can be laid on management: lack of genuine interest and follow-up.

One of the quality circle pioneers in the U.S., Hughes Aircraft now views circles as part of its corporate culture. Ten years of quality circles at Hughes led Circles' Corporate Manager Bill Courtright to write of an "improved management style . . . necessary for successful circles and for developing a company climate that encourages individual motivation, creativity, and . . . responsibility."[2]

There is no question that the Hughes circles were highly successful in saving money, eliminating defects, and improving efficiency. They also improved the climate of *Attention to quality* at Hughes. "It is impossible to document the savings that now result simply because employees who have participated in quality circles routinely communicate with supervisors before problems grow to significant proportions. The quality circle has fostered interest, commitment, and a habit of communicating which eliminates or reduces numerous problems."[3]

### Tandem Computers: Building Success With a Philosophical Climate

"All people are good."[4] The first of Jim Treybig's management principles for running Tandem Computers, in Cupertino, CA. A big assumption, but it worked. Tandem's strategy was to grow to major league status, while retaining the inspiring cultural aspects of its origins.

Tandem's weekly TGIF beer busts, company swimming pool, stock options for every employee, six-week sabbaticals every four years, not only created company commitment, but fit into the overall corporate philosophy of encouraging self-growth and developing human potential. These were fairly common incentives in Silicon Valley, where talent was always in demand. But all these attractions were a standard part of the environment, rather than perks.

The Tandem climate was further built by what *Fortune* magazine referred to as an "endless stream of company-boosting propaganda urging loyalty, hard work, self-esteem, and respect for co-workers." There was also the company's growth and strategy plan entitled "Understanding Our Philosophy," required reading for each employee. Tandem executives felt that showing everyone in the company the five-year plan and some strategic secrets would boost loyalty.

And it did. The company's engineering operations manager said, "I can't describe it, but it feels pretty good. I feel like I'm accomplishing something with myself."[5]

Could Tandem afford to put so much of its resources into something as intangible as the climate of the workplace? A better question might be: Could their competitors afford not to?

## Building Projects *The Rouse Way*

Ask people at The Rouse Company about the source of their success and you'll hear about doing things *The Rouse way*. Before long you pick up an air of enthusiasm and excellence—sensing this *Rouse way* without quite knowing what it is. It seems to come from a willingness to question everything Rouse people do, asking deep questions not only of their projects, but of their own process and values and themselves.

They begin looking at a problem in an idealistic way, but before it's over and done, they get into a very realistic, hard, bottom-line approach. "We try for a balance," says Laurin "Monk" Askew, vice-president and director of Design. "We look at problem solving from the user's standpoint rather than from our need to make it keep our own process intact. We make a real effort to solve the real problems—how it fits into the real world."

According to Bruce Armiger, vice-president and director of Construction, "We establish a forum for input from all aspects of the company, taking those interests and putting them all into the blend. It always amazes both newcomers and contractors to see how far we will go to achieve something that will seem extremely minor to an outsider, if we think it's important to doing the project the Rouse way—bringing quality and practicality together. We expend an inordinate amount of hours—many, many times more hours than our competitors do—to make our projects the very best they can be."

John Noggle, vice-president and senior development director, explains, "We're always building on what's happened. What was good about one project is carried over to another, and maybe what was not so good is not carried over. We never quit changing—each project is different. The company lets the team of people become very entrepreneurial. By the same token, you don't operate all by yourself in a vacuum. There are checks and balances, to make sure there's a lot of collective wisdom in what you're doing—and all of that thrown into the soup makes the projects come out well. It's the way the company's managed that makes the individual teams really responsible for the project. They all come together to make the project work."

How does The Rouse Company teach a new manager *The Rouse way?* They invest time in people just like they do in their projects. They put them in the Rouse climate to develop. Bruce Armiger explains, "As soon as somebody comes to work for us, we start putting him in meetings that don't have anything to do with his particular project, so he can begin to learn what is important to The Rouse Company. In a meeting of a project he will never work on, he learns by the conversation the importance we put on different things, what we feel is important. He'll learn it from all the people; everyone will tell newcomers about it. It's not so easy to learn."

"You learn it from experience," John Noggle reports. "It was absolutely foreign to me. I had always worked in a position where I made the decisions and set the direction without much input and was very traditional in the way I approached things. The influences on me were more external than internal. At Rouse, I found a whole collection of people, each very good in his own discipline. And unlike a lot of other companies, they're here to make the project as good as it can be, they're committed to the projects like I am. Personally, I had trouble learning to call on those other people to be responsible for the project, not just their own area. I've been learning to manage with consensus rather than being the sole decision maker. It's that whole sense of philosophy that was difficult for me to adjust to. Everyone has made it their job to help me get into the swing of things here."

Francie Connelly, executive secretary, tells how *The Rouse way* is fostered. "The company involves you in the projects. Being involved in the projects and being a part of the whole process enables you to understand the Rouse purpose and goals, and that makes you feel you're contributing—it's a worthwhile feeling."

Goodman concludes, "We are all well compensated here, but I don't think dollars would make nine-tenths of us work as hard as we do for the company and care as much as we do for the company if it wasn't for the way we work here and the excellence of the projects. When you go home at night, you know you've been working on the best projects in the country. And that makes everyone work harder, care more, work more intently to do it right. It keeps you from letting petty ideas get in the way of doing what's right for the job. You just feel good working here because of what we do and how we do it. That's why everybody has a desire to keep the Rouse way going."

You might call it integrity, defined as: (1) meeting self-set standards; (2) being whole or undivided. This climate of *The Rouse way* is the Managing By Influence leverage that Senior Vice-President Bruce Alexander needs to manage the division. He lives and breathes *The Rouse way* everyday, promoting it in every interaction. Is it worth his time and effort? He couldn't do his job without it.

### IBM: The First "THINK Tank"

When Thomas Watson Sr. took over the company that was to become IBM, every office and at times every desk displayed a sign that said "THINK," so the employee, not the visitor, could see it. Not only was it encouragement to be thoughtful and use good judgement when making decisions, it also served as a reminder of Watson's constant admonitions for hard work, company loyalty, and innovation. The author of a 1940 *Fortune* article said of Watson, "Let him discourse on the manifest destiny of IBM, and you are ready to join the company for life . . . Everybody in the organization is expected to find the ubiquitous THINK sign a constant source of inspiration, as the weary travelers of old found new strength in the wayside crucifixes."[6]

Watson couldn't personally reach everybody as the company grew, but his signs were everywhere. In offices, conference rooms, everywhere, THINK signs carried his message. He gave lectures on THINK and on loyalty to IBM, devoting time to establishing this company spirit. THINK signs did much more than send an individual message to each employee; at any moment, they created a climate at IBM. As much as it was misunderstood by outsiders, it was appreciated by the people who mattered, the people who carried out Watson's mission. While the country poked fun at THINK, the company built a loyal work force that led to success for the company and for themselves.

Both Watson and his son, Tom Watson Jr., did everything in their power to foster the super-ordinate goals of customer service, excellence, respect for the individual. It's easy to see that adherence to these principles is responsible for the success of IBM.

Today the THINK signs are rare, but the philosophies the Watsons espoused are still taught in "boot camp," IBM's introductory training sessions for new employees. And after eighteen years with the company, Bob Andrejko still knows them. He says, "We do keep in mind the philosophy to offer the 'best customer service in the world'—for example, even it it means changing products until a customer is satisfied. We do try to live by it, realistically blending it into all our work."

Bob Sisson, a marketing representative at the IBM Sacramento, CA, office says the philosophies ultimately are a yardstick around which to measure things. The point is, the climate that the founder created still exists and is recognized as a main contributor to the excellence of IBM.

## Marriott: The Detail Game

Chambermaids must follow sixty-six prescribed steps in making up a room. Cooks must not deviate from recipes without written permission. This attention to detail has equated the name Marriott with quality, and accounts for the success of the giant hotel and food services company.

It began with J. Willard Marriott. The story is told that for more than fifty years, he read every single customer complaint card, not just a summary of complaints prepared for him by his staff. The impact of this use of influence? All his managers worked very hard to make sure the boss had a very light reading load.

Hotel and restaurant visitors have come to expect the high quality standards set by top management. When things aren't quite right, the situation is corrected with no questions asked—just because Marriott stands for perfection and quality.

This climate of *Attention to details* is preserved by Marriott's top managers, who spend more than half the year on the road visiting company facilities and even learning how to cook in a company kitchen. They get daily operations reports and meet frequently with company managers. The result: an annual earnings growth rate near 20 percent.

## Hewlett-Packard: A Changing Climate

In the beginning, there were Bill (Hewlett) and Dave (Packard) and all the innovative young engineers they encouraged to be entrepreneurs within the company, sharing ideas in a fairly informal setting. The company grew to be very successful, its corporate culture legendary. But one hallmark was also Hewlett-Packard's fiercely autonomous divisions.

Competition (spelled IBM) forced Hewlett-Packard to consolidate some of those divisions and market to a wider audience. President and CEO John Young focused the new corporate strategy on quality. These are some of the ways he said a CEO can foster quality improvement:

–Dramatize the importance of quality: convince people there are always better ways to do things.

–Establish agreed-upon measures of quality.

–Set motivating goals and don't be afraid to use peer competition.

–Reward results.

–Maintain the attitude that high quality is not only desirable, but possible.[7]

Could Young be there in every situation to contribute to quality? Of course not; but he could make his presence felt throughout the climate he worked to create.

### Iacocca's "New Chrysler Company"

Until November, 1978, Chrysler was Chrysler. Then, Chrysler became Lee Iacocca. The automaker made money again and put people back to work. And even though Iacocca credited the people who helped him turn the company around, it was he who was bold enough to create a new image for Chrysler. He became a folk hero.

He maintained morale even while cutting payroll and closing plants. He began working side by side with the UAW. He took a well-publicized salary cut to one dollar a year. And he put his face on TV, gambling that the American public would once again come through on the side of the underdog.

Lee Iacocca created the climate, *We Can Do It*. Those words were inscribed on a sign at the plant that began making the K-car. When the first car rolled off the line, another sign was added underneath, saying *Consider It Done*. Iacocca was the ultimate promoter. But perhaps his most important promoting was done inside Chrysler, to create a climate of perseverance and winning.

# 6

# Promoting Commitment

## EIGHT SECRETS ABOUT COMMITMENT

William Ouchi said organizations are social beings and their success depends on trust, subtlety and intimacy.[1] This doesn't diminish the need for practicality in the hard facts of business, planning, and control, but rather it focuses well-deserved attention on the nature of the vehicle that produces the results—the organization itself.

No matter how automated and systematized they are, organizations remain social beings. The heart of this matter of trust, subtlety and intimacy is commitment. And commitment is often misunderstood or not understood at all. No organizational experience is more powerful or more subtle. While commitment is difficult to describe or explain, people live with it everyday. Everyone measures it and relates to others based on perceptions of their commitment. Trust and intimacy relate directly to the experience of commitment.

### 1. People Avoid Commitment

It doesn't have four letters, but to many people commitment is a dirty word. When thinking about their commitments, they feel suppressed, oppressed, or put upon.

How about you? Suppose a good friend asks you to go to

the movies and you say you'd like that. Suppose the friend then proposes a date that's three weeks away? How would you typically respond? Most people would ask to make it tentative, arranging to call each other about a week ahead of time. They like to keep their options open.

Making that commitment to the movies ties you down. After all, what if something more important comes along? Maybe you'll have to work late. Perhaps you'll have put in a big week and be tired or want to spend some time with your kids. The point is, if you make a commitment with honor, your whole life revolves around it. So everyone has some tendency to avoid commitment.

### 2. Commitment Exists in Duality

To understand commitment, you first have to understand the nature of life itself: Nothing exists without the coexistent experience of its absence. In some cases this absence is its opposite, but only the absence is needed.

In simple talk, you can't have "day" without "night." Night is the absence of day. If night ceased to exist, day would be gone as well. Day is defined by night, and night is defined by day.

You can't have "up" without "down." Many people think of up and down as opposites, but down can be looked on as the absence of up. (Of course, up can be seen as the absence of down, as well.) One makes the other. Each one's existence depends on the other's coexistence.

Think about the following question for a moment before reading on. What name do you give to the sound that began before you were born and has continued constantly, never varying, the whole time you've been alive? That is, you weren't alive before this sound began, and it hasn't changed or varied throughout your life. What do you call that sound?

The sound described has never been absent in your life. Therefore, it would not exist for you. What do you call the sound which doesn't exist? You call it silence. To verify this, think of a time when you were in an air-conditioned room all day and the air conditioner was turned off. You suddenly noticed a strange new sound: "absence of air conditioner." You then realized that you had long since "stopped hearing" the air conditioner. It had become your base level experience, which you call silence: the absence of sound.

When Oriental philosophers speak of this "existence/absence" nature of life, they call it the yin-yang of reality, or duality.

### 3. You Can't Have 100 Percent Commitment

Since nothing can exist without the coexistence of its absence, we now come to the saddest truth in life: Life can never be all holidays. If life were all holidays, there would be no holidays. You know this for yourself—you need to have workdays to have holidays. Even as a kid you knew that. People who retire find this out all too harshly. It's not just a clever saying, it's reality.

Suppose there were 364 holidays in a year, and one workday. How would people treat the workday? There would probably be a big Macy's Workday Parade in New York City. Folks would go out and get special workday clothes, new each year. Advertisers would let them know how many days were left until Workday. People would send each other cards. The workday would become more important than the holidays.

It's a fact of life: one thing demands its absence to have existence. This is not empty philosophy, it's a basic truth about life. Understanding it will make you a better leader. It opens the door to understanding commitment. No one can be 100 percent committed to anything. That experience cannot exist. If there were no experience of noncommitment, there could not be any experience of commitment.

### 4. It's Okay That No One Is 100 Percent Committed

Are these mere words, or are they the truth? Look to your own life to make that determination. Is there anyone who wouldn't leave your organization under the right circumstances? Wouldn't you leave if the right conditions came to pass? Take the person whom you perceive as the most committed to your organization, whether it's you or someone else. Think of some situation under which this person would leave.

Perhaps he'd leave for the health of a family member who must go to another climate or somewhere for special medical care. Maybe he'd go if offered some important job by the President of the United States, where all financial guarantees were made and the call to the nation's need was great. Or maybe he'd take a different position if it offered more challenge or ten times the pay or six months off each year—the dream job. While it may take a stretch of your imagination to picture yourself or someone else leaving, realize that there is that possibility—not just in theory, but in reality.

In short, if the best job that you could possibly imagine comes along, you might leave what you're doing. Does that mean you aren't committed where you are? Not at all. You are committed and if something extraordinary comes along, you might leave. You could leave and still express your commitment. You could give a lot of notice, find your replacement, make sure everyone else had a good deal, leave things in great shape. You could make sure others could contact you in the future. You could leave as if your leaving were part of your job—because you are committed.

Some people are afraid to see that they are not 100 percent committed. Perhaps they fear they will become irresponsible if they admit their noncommitment. To be an effective leader, it's important to recognize that there can be an experience of commitment only when the experience of noncommitment also exists. Without the noncommitment, the commitment is a pretense.

On the other hand, and far less obvious, noncommitment cannot exist without the experience of commitment. No one can be zero percent committed either. This point is more subtle and more powerful. It permits you to take a position of common interest with everyone else in your company.

## 5. It Works to Take a Useful Point of View

To best understand this issue of commitment and non-commitment, first look at the nature of clocks. Clocks make a sound: tick tock tick tock tick tock tick tock. Most people agree that a clock goes *tick tock*. They've heard that since they were kids. So it's a fact that clocks go tick tock tick tock tick tock tick tock, and people say a clock goes "tick tock."

But who's to say a clock doesn't go *tock tick?* You could argue that a clock goes tock tick, couldn't you? In fact, if the person who invented clocks had pushed the pendulum the other way first, we'd have clocks that go tock tick. It's easy to argue either way, tick tock or tock tick. Both are correct, and the one you prefer is only your point of view or attitude. So, whether it's *tick tock* or *tock tick* is up to you, the chooser, to determine.

Duality asserts that life, like a clock, has a tick tock nature: existence/absence. You can think of the tick tock of life as: yes no yes no yes no yes no yes no yes no. You can't have something without having its absence at the same time, and *no* is the absence of *yes*. However, people usually say *yes but* instead of *yes no*. The *but* takes the place of *no* in representing the absence of *yes*. You couldn't have the *yes* without the *but*.

Just as with tick tock and tock tick, *yes but* or *but yes* is only a point of view. Both are accurate, but they give a different emphasis. See what happens when you are asked these questions.

–Are you a good son or daughter?

–Are you a good manager?

–Are you a good citizen?

Most people answer, "Yes, but . . ." The "but" focuses on the part of them that is not 100 percent. For example: "Yes, I'm a good son, *but* I could call home more often, I don't listen so well, and sometimes I just resist my parents for no good reason." Or, "Yes, I'm a good manager, *but* I don't acknowledge people enough, I'm not organized enough, and I don't listen well enough." Or, "Yes, I'm a good citizen, *but* I do speed, and I have cut a few corners on my income tax."

For most people, the overriding personal experience of life has a *yes but* focus. That is, they recognize the positive but usually have a lingering focus on the "unpositive," or negative. Ask most people if they are satisfied with life, and you'll get, "Yes, *but* . . ."

The same goes for commitment. Ask most people if they are committed to the place they work and you'll get, "Yes, but . . ." More important, ask most managers if their people are committed to the company and you'll get, "Yes, but . . ." This makes sense since no one is 100 percent committed or zero percent committed. So there's a *yes* and a *but* and the choice between *yes but* or *but yes* is still only a point of view. However, look at the difference. Which is more useful for the leader to focus on—the part that's not committed or the part that is committed? Obviously, the part that is committed. But yes!

The French have a saying, "Mais oui!" — "But yes!" The same two words, with a very different focus and meaning. It's only a point of view.

### 6. You Can Lead by Focusing on Commitment

You may have been reluctant in the past to acknowledge the commitment of your people to the company because you see a big piece of the *but* and not much of the *yes*. However, the name of the game is "Follow the Leader," not "Follow the Follower." It is the leader's job to go first. You have the choice of which to focus on. If you focus on the commitment you and your people have to the organization, you'll be dealing with the truth of the situation in a way that promotes commitment. If you focus on the lack of commitment, you'll be dealing with the truth in a way that fosters cynicism and retards commitment.

It's your job to see the commitment in your people, to relate to it, express it, promote it, and bring it out. It's not their job to go first. You took the job as leader so it's your job to go first.

George S. Patton was a great general. Talking to his men before a major battle, he might have said, "Men, we're going out, and we're going to win. We're going to uphold the honor of our country. We're going to protect our families. Men, I know you care about this the way I care about it. We're going to win, and nothing is going to stop us because *we are committed* to our country, and *we are committed* to history."

Do you think it ever occurred to Patton that at least some of the men he was talking to may not have been committed? Yet he didn't get up and say, "Look, fellas, I know a lot of you are probably less than 100 percent committed to this, and I'm asking something of you that is extraordinary. I hope you'll think about your commitment to your country." Not at all. Patton focused on and related to the part of the soldiers that was "But yes!" He related to that commitment with such intensity that around Patton soldiers *were committed*. He kept the spotlight on the commitment, not on the noncommitment. He saw it even when it wasn't evident to anyone else, even to the soldiers themselves.

Leaders must understand that their people are committed, even though not 100 percent. It doesn't matter whether people are committed more or less, as long as, while they are together, they relate to one another through the part of them that is committed.

## 7. Assuming No Commitment: A Manager's Pitfall

It has been said that "unexpressed competence appears much the same as incompetence."[2] This implies that management normally presumes incompetence unless competence is specifically shown. Therefore, managers work to defend their companies against incompetence and act to instill competence instead of just letting it surface naturally from workers.

The same description applies to management's assumption about workers' commitment. Unexpressed commitment appears much the same as noncommitment. Leaders can de-

fend against the lack of commitment or can recognize that it
lies below the surface, unexpressed, until the climate is right
for its expression. Whether you can see it or not, your people
are committed. Even if you can't see it in any given instance,
the only useful point of view is to assume they are committed.

Sometimes you find people who will not express their
commitment under any circumstances. Perhaps their fear or
selfishness precludes this expression. Even though you understand the duality of commitment, you may find it impossible
to bring forth the person's experience and expression of commitment. Once you come to this point with an employee,
where all you can see is that the person is zero percent committed (100 percent noncommitted), there's only one alter-
native: turn that person loose. If an individual is 100 percent
noncommitted to working for your company, you cannot deal
with him and cannot have a commitment to him.

### *Self-Check*

*Take a moment to consider how you deal with commit-
ment.*

> *–Think of someone who has never openly
> expressed a commitment to your
> organization. Ask yourself: Do I treat
> that person as if he or she is committed?*
>
> *–Recall someone who never said much
> about being committed to your
> organization but later came through to
> prove a real commitment. Ask yourself:
> Did I expect it? Did I do anything to
> bring it out?*
>
> *–Ask yourself: Have I ever assumed a
> commitment in someone who usually
> said he or she wasn't really committed?
> What was the outcome?*

Managers often act as though it's part of their job to
instill commitment in people, to put it there. That's silly. It's

management's job to *promote* the commitment that already exists. Workers are unhappy when their commitment is not honored or when it is suppressed. You make a person's work fulfilling by relating to his or her commitment. Even if a worker avoids experiencing or expressing commitment, as most people normally do, the leader can evoke the commitment by treating the person as if he or she *is* committed. Sure there's some risk, but to assume noncommitment is a self-fulfilling prophesy you can't afford.

A Giant Food zone director recalls N. M. Cohen, Izzy Cohen's father and one of the founders of Giant Food. "N. M. believed that management was responsible for keeping all associates as honest on the job as they were when they were hired. He believed that everyone we hire is honest, and when they come on board it's our responsibility to keep them honest—to educate them about how important it is to their welfare to be honest." It's no coincidence that people were honest around N. M. Cohen.

---

### MBI ACTIONS

**#42.** Observe the way you relate to one particular person whom you feel is not committed to your organization. Notice whether your actions are leading that person to behavior which reinforces your original feelings about him or her.

**#43.** Now, focus instead on that employee's commitment, however small it may appear at first. See if your actions toward that employee change, perhaps in a way that encourages him or her to express more commitment.

---

### 8. People Are Naturally Committed

It's in people's nature to be committed. Even those who would deny having much commitment to anything turn out to have commitments to some of the oddest things. They will argue over the merits of Chevrolets and Fords, going beyond logic to a heartfelt care, concern, and commitment for the well-being of these corporate giants.

People are naturally committed beings. They always want to be part of a group. Being sensitive to the commitment of your people is an unusually valuable leadership skill. Even as you listen to people who tell you, "Aw, I just work here, it's just a job," you can still see their commitment. People have a warm place in their hearts for their companies.

## SIX BENEFITS OF PROMOTING COMMITMENT

Every year, millions of quarter-inch drill bits are sold. And yet, nobody wants a quarter-inch drill bit; they all want a quarter-inch hole. Commitment is the same way. While it's interesting to talk about commitment, how does it affect the bottom line? That's the important question and only you can answer it for your company. Take some time to read about companies that attribute their success largely to the commitment of their people. You can consider whether the results for your company are worth your efforts.

### 1. Commitment Relates to Trust: "Where's He Coming From?"

When people listen to each other, they don't listen only to the words. They first listen to hear the other person's motives. They ask themselves: "Where's he coming from? What's her motive? Why is she telling me that? Who's he looking out for? Can I trust her?"

Then, they take what they were told, filter it through the screen that's appropriate for the other person's motivation, and respond. Even in the smallest matter, people check for motivation. When someone tells you that you look nice today, you don't accept it until you determine the person has no ulterior motive, such as getting on your good side or acting like a goody-goody. Have you ever been to a clothing shop where the salesperson remarked on everything the customer touched, "Oh, that would look terrific on you!" Whose interest is being served?

## Self-Check

*Give thought to your own attitudes about where people are coming from and what they're committed to. Ask yourself:*

- *–If someone is talking with me as if something is for the good of the company, but I suspect it's really in his or her own personal interest, how do I react? Does it make me cynical?*

- *–When this happens, do I respond to the issues the person is discussing, or am I affected more by the person's motives?*

- *–If I know someone is talking from the common commitment we share for the company, do I find myself more open and trusting? Do I then respond to the issues, satisfied that the discussion can be open and honest?*

## 2. Commitment Aids Conflict Resolution

What do you do when two people have a difference they can't reconcile, and they come to you for resolution? How do you come out "clean," without favoritism, without their resenting you, and without resentment between the conflicting parties?

The resolution of any conflict lies in the discovery of common ground. Once all parties find a mutual interest, they can resolve their differences. Most people look for personal common ground with others. By definition, that doesn't exist. Each person's own personal ground is unique. So, to find common ground, people must look beyond themselves.

When two people come to you for assistance in resolving differences, they each assume they have common ground with you; each trusts you to act on a basis larger than your own personality. (If people don't come to you for conflict resolution, ask yourself The Question of Influence to learn why.) They don't trust each other but each has a trusting relationship with you which produces some common ground. Think back to Chapter 3 with Jeff Peck and his two managers who couldn't get along.

Peck assumed they did have common interest, even though they didn't recognize it. He only had to ask each one, "Are you willing to act in the best interest of the company?" They both were and started to work on that basis. Peck maintained their intraorganizational relationship whenever trouble popped up by reminding them they had each proven to the other that they would act for the good of the company once they were reminded. As time passed, the moments when the two men lost sight of their common interest became infrequent.

At NS&T Bank in Washington, DC, senior vice-presidents find they can resolve any disagreement with a simple dialogue that might go as follows: *VP 1:* "Well, is your way for the good of the bank?" *VP 2:* "Hold it a second, let me take another look at that." After some thought, *VP 2 might say,* "Yes, what I said was for the good of the bank," or it might be, "You're absolutely right. What I said was not for the good of the bank; it was for the good of my department. Fine. We'll do it your way." That kind of exchange is invaluable: it saves resources and breaks logjams.

### *Self-Check*

*How do you help people work through conflict? Ask yourself:*

> —*When two people come to me to resolve a problem, what logic do I apply?*
>
> —*Where do I look to achieve resolution?*
>
> —*What criteria do I use to judge my effectiveness?*

Isn't the answer to all three of these questions the same? You ask yourself, "What's best for the company?" Then you ask them to come together for this common interest. If one of the people won't do this, you don't have a problem between two people but you do have an issue with the one person. You may need to ask him to step out of character. And very likely, that means you'll have to step out of character first by asking him. But remember, you're the leader, and leaders go first.

---

### — MBI ACTIONS —

**#44.** When you do apply this common interest to conflict resolution, let your people know. Tell them that the company interest is the basis of all work in the company. This will give them the ability to resolve conflicts without you, and it will further their experience of the committed working relationship everyone shares at the company. Soon, they'll start doing it without coming to you. They usually already know what's best for the company—they just haven't thought about it in this situation.

---

### 3. Commitment Accelerates Decision Making and Problem Solving

When a decision or problem comes to you from your staff, very often the critical element you add is the answer to the question, "What's best for the company?" If your people knew how to apply this question and its answer, they could work matters out without you.

Enhance their ability to make decisions and to solve problems without you by using each instance as a learning process. When you gather the information to solve a problem, ask your staff, "What do you think would be in the best interest of the company?" After all, that's what you do, isn't it? Sometimes that's all you add to the solution since they already have the answers and other information. When they hear your thought process enough and learn what you think is best for the company, they'll begin to make more decisions without you and bring you problems *and* solutions, or just carry on without letting you know.

---
## MBI ACTIONS
---

**#45.** Help your people take on more decision making and problem solving by teaching them your thought process and by giving them more of the information they require to consider the overall company needs. Don't keep your thoughts and thought process a mystery. There's no leverage in that.

**#46.** If you find they need a lot of information they don't have, hold a seminar where you can share more information with them about the good of the company. This will enable them to solve more problems and make more decisions without you. Discuss past decisions made and problems solved. Let them interview you until they understand how you arrived at your solutions. If you find inconsistencies in your own process, you can make adjustments. This meeting will do more than educate your staff. It will also educate you about yourself.

---

### 4. Commitment Ends a *Protect-Your-Turf* Climate

People protect their own turf when they don't sense the safety of common turf. No one is 100 percent free from this attitude of self-protection but some are more prone to it than others. As the leader, you can use potent leverage by building a climate of common commitment which lessens the perceived need to "take care of number one."

As your people *perceive* common interest, they will naturally begin *acting* for the common good. Although some people may require more explicit leadership than others, you'll be surprised that many will respond to implicit managing by influence, sometimes without realizing it themselves. Therefore, as the leader, you must keep a close eye on people to acknowledge their movement away from protecting their turf. Be careful to use the phrase "in the past" when observing your hard-core cases. Don't be the one to hold them back by relating to their old ways.

You can develop common ground in an organization by

reversing a popular term used in business. Many people talk about *interpersonal relations in organizations*. Turn that around and look at the potent experience that comes from *intraorganizational relations among persons*.

It brings the appropriate relationship into focus: intra-organizational. People don't come to work at your company for interpersonal reasons. They work together for intra-organizational reasons. However, they're not like parts of a machine—they're persons and have personal commitments other than the commitment they share at the company. Every one of them has that basic commitment to their own egos known as personalities. But by focusing on their intra-organizational role, they can go beyond their personalities. If they all came together for nothing more than their own personal motives, you'd have anarchy.

### 5. Commitment Cures a Cynic

A cynic believes human conduct is motivated exclusively by self-interest. No one is 100 percent cynical, but some people have a prevailing attitude that all others are moti-vated wholly out of self-interest.

There are times when it's wise to be cynical. If a stranger approached you with a gun, you'd be very cynical. It would be clear that he or she was acting out of self-interest. From time to time, everyone acts in self-interest to the exclusion of mu-tual interest, so people are justified in being cynical on occasion.

The trouble comes when someone's underlying attitude smacks of cynicism. This outlook colors everything the cynic observes. As a result, cynics also operate out of self-interest, not trusting others to act for the common good. This makes them hard to relate to and tends to spoil the climate for oth-ers. Cynics are a challenge to the experience and expression of commitment to the organization. As such, cynics have a se-vere detrimental effect with the same potent leverage of in-fluence that you are using, only in the reverse direction.

Everyone wants to know how to change cynics. Here's the

key: don't try to change their personalities. You can lead people out of cynicism by creating a climate of commitment
around them. Then ask them to step out of character—ask
them to acknowledge that the people around them are working for the good of the company. Lead them to see the intra-
organizational relationship they share with others. Ask them
to discover an organizational trust that exists in their "companality" that hasn't existed in the past in their "personality."

Don't deny that people are sometimes justified in being
cynical. Show them, however, that there are other times when
cynicism is inappropriate. Help them see that they do care
deeply for the organization and that their cynicism isn't best
for the company. They need to change their own point of view
about themselves, from one of being a cynic who sometimes
doesn't act cynically to one of being a noncynic who sometimes acts cynically. *Yes but* or *but yes:* it's all a point of view.
Since YOU CAN NEVER NOT LEAD, see which point of
view is best for you to take with the person who, in the past,
acted like a cynic.

Apply The Question of Influence to see how you've reinforced the cynic's self-image. Nobody really wants to be a
cynic; everyone wants to be able to trust and relax. The discovery that everyone around him is committed to the same
thing (the company) gives the cynic a basis from which to
supersede his own personal interest and re-examine his underlying cynicism. For people whose personalities have run to
cynicism in the past, it may be one of the rare chances to step
out of character and be trusting. It could change their whole
lives.

### 6. Commitment Builds to Communication

It's vital to have *open* communication. The success of any
organization is limited by the quality of its communication. It
must be unguarded communication that constantly comes toward you, as opposed to guarded, careful communication that
you need to pull out of people.

The communication must be *direct,* not the kind where

you need to talk around the matter, walking on eggshells and being afraid of offending. Rather, the quality must be, "Please don't take this personally, I don't mean it personally." This doesn't disregard the need for sensitivity, but rather permits business talk with a frankness we don't often have in personal talk. This honesty applies not only to negative feedback, but to positive words as well. Most people can't take compliments, so it's just as important to have your listener not take your positive comments personally, either. You want your people to know what they do well for the good of the organization. After all, you want them to do more of those things more often!

You can use commitment as the base of open, direct *company* communication. This doesn't address personal communication, but reflects back to intraorganizational relations between persons, not interpersonal relations in organizations.

People must be sensitive to the reality that organizations are made of persons, and persons have toes that get stepped on, feelings that get hurt, and personalities that conflict. However, you can lead your organization to the conscious pursuit of a climate that builds relationships on the organizational ties while honoring its employees' humanity and human foibles. After all, it's in the best interest of the organization to take care of its people.

This open, direct, company communication follows a path of dependent steps. Communication depends on *rapport*. If you don't have rapport, you don't have communication. Rapport means a relationship marked with harmony, accord, and affinity. If two people have a relationship marked with disharmony and discord, they won't communicate. They may talk and exchange information, but communication is more than that.

Communication is the deep exchange of experience that brings the two parties to a full understanding of each other, including the understanding that they understand each other. People actually go out of their way to *not* communicate with people with whom they feel out of harmony.

Rapport depends on *trust*. If you don't have trust, you

have a relationship marked with distrust and cynicism. You remain guarded. As discussed earlier, trust depends on *commitment*. When determining trust for someone, you ask, "What is this person committed to?"

### The Path to Communication
**COMMUNICATION**
Depends On
**RAPPORT**
Depends On
**TRUST**
Depends On
**COMMITMENT**

The path to communication leads to one of the most rewarding benefits of commitment: open, direct, company communication. Like any genuine communication, it is effective, nurturing and fulfilling. The quality of people's communication at work can be the highest in their lives and can contribute to their ability to communicate elsewhere.

While communication requires two people, it takes only one to lead the way down the path. If one person is willing to be responsible for recalling common commitment, it's possible to establish trust and move into honest communication. In your role as a leader, by recognizing common commitment, common trust, and the existing rapport, you can *lead* others to communication. By your own act of open, direct, company communication, you will evoke the experience of being committed because you will have demonstrated your own trust, and hence your commitment.

Focus on the commitment in your people and communicate with them showing your trust. If someone lets you down, you'll have adequate time to take action. Be a leader, going first and creating a climate of open, direct, company communication.

## RECOGNIZING HOW WORKING RELATIONSHIPS ARE MADE

A vice-president at NS&T Bank, call him Lew Jeffries, recalls an incident that throws light on the difference between interpersonal relations and intraorganizational relations. Jeffries says, "I came to understand about company commitment being the basis of our relationships at work. I worked with another vice-president, Bob, for twenty years. We had a nice, pleasant rapport. We worked well together and always enjoyed chatting about lots of things. Then Bob retired.

"He came back about six weeks later and said, 'Hi Lew, how are you?' I said, 'Fine, Bob. How are you?' And he said, 'Fine . . . how are you?' And I said, 'I'm doing well . . . how about you?' Then, after an awkward pause, I asked him about his golf game. It turned out that we had little in common in the past that didn't have to do with the bank. While we knew some personal things about each other, for all those years our whole relationship was based on the bank.

"We both felt uncomfortable now. It was more than just lacking something to say. There just wasn't the old thread of rapport, even after twenty years."

———

Suppose you go out to a football game on a Sunday afternoon in Chicago; the Bears are playing. You see two people in the row ahead of you who came in with single seats, not knowing anyone else there. Under normal circumstances, you might conclude that these two would find little in common since one is a woman, the other a man; one is black, the other white; one has a Southern accent, the other an Eastern accent; one is middle-aged, the other young. They sit there facing the field, not even saying hello.

On the third play of the game, the referee makes a call against the Bears that the players protest. The partisan fans begin yelling and booing. In the excitement, the two people in front of you both stand up. She calls out, "You're blind, ref. You blew it!" He yells, "Are you their twelfth player?" They look at each other and realize that they're both Bears fans. They have something very important in common when they're going to a Bears game. They have a Bears commitment. Bears trust. Bears rapport. And they can have Bears communication. In no time they're talking up a storm, having a great time.

When the game ends, they say a quick goodbye, one turns to the right, the other to the left, and they walk out. They have nothing else in common, nothing to communicate about. As they see each other moments later on the way out, they both seem to avoid the other, not feeling comfortable without the rapport built by their enthusiasm for the game. The basis of their relationship was the Bears relationship.

It's like that at work. You don't need to have a strong personal relationship with people. That's not necessary. You don't need to be the same in any way except one: That you are committed to the same thing. Around that, because of that, you can have terrific communication, rapport, and trust. With this shared commitment, you can keep matters in perspective—relationships and decisions become more rational. The foundation is, "Well, what's in the best interest of the company?"

---

## MBI ACTIONS

**#47.** Find someone in your organization whom you don't know well and haven't talked to much in the past. Strike up a conversation about the organization, treating the person as if you both had something in common (you do). Notice how easy it is to talk company business and how it leaves a relationship in place.

---

### HOW TO HANDLE CONFLICTING COMMITMENTS

People are committed to many things: to their ego; to their family; to their sex, their race, their religion; to their country; even to global ideals. Does that negate or take away from their commitment to their company? Absolutely not.

People who work together often form personal relationships with one another. Sometimes people come to work for a company because friends who work there brought them in. But your leadership potency will be enhanced when you recognize that the reason you're all together is not these other relationships—it's the company relationship.

Your people have myriad relationships: male relationships; female relationships; single people relationships; married people relationships; older folks relationships, and so on. As real as those likenesses and differences are, they are not the basis on which they come together. When an individual comes to work for a company, he or she doesn't need to have any special personal relationships; it's enough that there be a willingness to be a company employee. As the leader, your attitude toward these various commitments sets the climate. To handle conflicting commitments, recognize the potential for conflict and keep the one common umbrella—commitment to the organization—in view at all times.

## FOUR STEPS LEADING TO COMMITMENT

First, beware of the self-fulfilling prophesy that your people are not committed. Examine your thoughts and attitudes regarding this issue. Your behavior will follow this attitude and that behavior will lead your people to noncommitment.

Second, use The Question of Influence to find the part you play in the present state of commitment. Ask the question of yourself and your people. Put it on your calendar, making the issue of commitment and your influence high priority items. Tackle the matter of commitment as if it were vitally important to your company—it is.

Third, take a useful point of view, even when you can't seem to find any commitment in your people, and you can't imagine how you could be responsible for the level of commitment. If you adopt the attitude that they are not committed and you can't do anything to bring out any commitment, you're left with no possible action and no potential. It's a useless point of view. Assume the commitment is there, and it only awaits your learning how to bring it out. Then you will take action. Even if you feel or look foolish, you know you're doing your best. And usually your best will get the job done.

Fourth, step out of character in your leadership efforts to promote commitment. You're often asking something of the people around you which has not been asked in the past. While it's becoming more common now, expressing commitment is still a major change for some people. Have empathy for them and lead them to it by having the humility to step out of character yourself. Don't lose sight of the inspiration you provide to your people. Remember: YOU CAN NEVER NOT LEAD. Use all you've got.

# 7

# Proven Commitment Strategies

There are 100 opportunities everyday to lead your company to the experience and expression of commitment. You can use them or you can let them go by. But since you're always leading, either consciously or unconsciously, you can't let these opportunities go by with impunity. Many executives and managers suppress commitment rather than evoke it. Apply The Question of Influence with Beginner's Mind to help you find your own impact.

*Self-Check*

*How are you at bringing out a company commitment in your people? Ask yourself:*

> *—Does my leadership promote a company commitment from my staff or a personal commitment?*
>
> *—Which do I respect and foster in my people?*
>
> *—Does my staff work for me or for the company?*

When you consider the immense underlying importance of company commitment, you see that you can't afford to give less than your best effort to promote it. It's worth your full force because it makes the rest of your work effective. If you do only one thing in your work, create a climate of commitment to the organization.

## TEN STRATEGIES TO PROMOTE COMMITMENT IN YOUR ORGANIZATION AND HOW TO IMPLEMENT THEM

These commitment strategies vary from informal moment-to-moment actions to formal policies and procedures. Some will lend themselves more readily to your organization and your style than others, but all can be used by adaptation and by stepping out of character. You may notice that you're using them now, even by omission. It won't take much on your part to implement them—mostly a greater awareness. In putting them to work, use all your normal management abilities and tools. Make plans, measure your results, and use management systems for follow-up. Use The Question of Influence for feedback on how you are doing.

### 1. Use "We" and "Our"

When talking about the organization and its accomplishments, managers often say "I" and "my." While this does express a valuable individual responsibility for your job, consider the effect it has on the climate of the workplace. "I" and "my" can exclude others from feeling it's also their organization. When you legitimately share responsibility for your organization with your people, you evoke a sense of ownership and commitment from them.

Using "we" and "our" won't work as a clever form of lip service. If you say these words but you're viewed as shallow because your actions belie the shared experience, then you'll breed cynicism. Consider the truth of the situation: Could you do your job without your people? If the answer is yes, get rid of your people. If the answer is no, then saying "we" and "our" will be telling the truth. If you normally would say, "I met my goals in my organization," recognize that you didn't do it alone. Change your words. See the difference it makes with your people.

This doesn't mean you can't ever say "I" or "my," only that everything you say affects the climate of your organization. And the climate *This is our organization* is more useful than *This is the boss's organization*. If you feel awkward at first, step out of character. If people notice the change and mention it, acknowledge that you recognize you haven't shared ownership with the rest of the people who make the organization work. You'll get their attention and be an inspiration to them to step out of character. If you now say "we" and "our" while your people use words like "I," "my," "they," and "theirs," ask The Question of Influence to learn how to lead them to more ownership.

---

### MBI ACTIONS

**#48.** Observe your own use of "I," "my," "we," and "our." As you notice you're using "I" and "my," switch to "we" and "our" and be aware of the influence you've gained in just that simple, minor difference. If it's uncomfortable, examine your attitudes toward the role your staff plays in the accomplishments of your organization.

---

### 2. Let People Know What You Honor

Don't assume that people know how much you respect them for their commitment to the company. Let them know you honor it. Be verbal even if you find it uncomfortable; step out of character. If you haven't been good at putting it into words in the past, learn how to do it. Give it as much effort and professionalism as you would a sales presentation to a prospect or a loan application to a bank. Treat it as serious business.

If people think you're corny, that's okay. Most people don't feel any more comfortable with the topic than you do. But that's a small price to pay for the results. Be like General Patton. Tell people, "Nothing's more important to me in an

employee or colleague than a commitment to the company."
When someone does something well, always express appreciation for the commitment in addition to thanks for a job done
well. Take time out to talk about commitment. Nothing shows
how much you honor an issue like the investment of your
time. You'll know you're getting your job done when you hear
others talking it up.

### 3. Don't Use "I'll Take Care of You; You Take Care of Me"

Many managers use an expedient way to create loyalty
from their workers. They make a private arrangement, sometimes implicit, that they will take care of the person if he or
she will take care of them. In the worst of cases, it's done to
the conscious detriment of the company, with the managers
trying to protect their own skin. But even in the best of cases,
where it's seen as a way to promote loyalty and enable managers to do a better job for the company, it still has bad effects.

While many managers do not explicitly make this arrangement with their people, they foster it by acts of omission—failure to actively establish common commitment to
the company as the basis of their working relationship with
their followers. This omission tends to promote "I'll take care
of you; you take care of me" by the subtle effects of the manager's influence. But this steals from the manager's power.

Suppose you made this type of deal with each of five
people working for you: Alice, Bob, Carl, Donna, and Edna.
They've all done their jobs well, thereby taking good care of
you and keeping their part of the bargain. One day Alice
walks into your office saying, "Well, I've taken good care of
you, now I need something from you. Fire Bob." Later that
day, Bob stops in to tell you, "I've taken care of you, so you
have to take care of me. Fire Alice." Now you're in a bind. You
have no leverage to get them together or to turn them down.
You have no power now to ask anything more.

Think how much more useful it would be to establish a
strong company relationship when you hire new people. Tell
them, "All I ask is that you have a loyalty to the company.

Any loyalty you have to me will come from the commitment we both share to the company. You don't need to work for my personal favor, just in a way that forwards the company and what it stands for. If we both do this, we'll get along fine. We can take care of each other in a way that allows us each to do the best job for the company. You can always come to me if you think I'm not fulfilling my part of the deal, and I'll come to you if I think you're not. This isn't a personal relationship we're building, although we do need to be sensitive to each other as people." If it suits your style you can add, "I do like to develop a personal relationship with my people, but it's not needed for your success here." Then you have power when Alice comes in to talk about Bob. You can treat their relationship as company business (which it is, anyway).

Not only does "I'll take care of you; you take care of me" hurt you in specific situations, it also takes away from the climate of company commitment. Promote your company relationship with your people in everything you do and in all the words you use. While it may seem to leave you more vulnerable to them, think about it this way: it's both the truth of why you are working together and a useful point of view.

### 4. Avoid *Personal* "Thank You's"

Even your "thank you's" say something, and they may be giving the wrong message. You can evoke commitment from your people by the way you thank them.

Suppose you have fallen behind in some paperwork and would like someone to work extra time to get it up-to-date. You might have the following conversation, although you would be implying the word *personally* most of the time rather than saying it. "Pete, I'd like to (personally) speak to you for a moment. I've (personally) gotten myself into a (personal) bind by (personally) falling behind in my (personal) job, and I'd like to ask a *personal* favor of you. Could you (personally) give me a hand by (personally) doing a little extra and (personally) saving me a lot of (personal) trouble? If you can (personally) do it, I'd *personally* appreciate it." When Pete is done, you say, "Pete, I *personally* thank you for helping me out! I knew I *personally* could count on you as usual."

While you wouldn't say *personally* all those times in parentheses, you'd often be meaning it, as if you have a right to ask Pete to do this for you personally but not for the company. And, people normally consider a *personal* "thank you" more valuable in showing appreciation than a plain "thanks" or a *company* "thank you." But see what you're promoting with the personal plea and acknowledgment.

Consider this conversation about the same matter. Just as above, some of the conversation is implicit, but notice the different flavor. "Pete, I'd like to speak to you for a moment (for the good of the company). I've gotten the company in a bind by falling behind in my (company) job, and I'd like to ask you, since I know you care about the company, to give a (company) hand by doing a little extra and saving the company a lot of trouble. If you can do it (for the good of the company), the *company* will appreciate it." When Pete is done, you say, "Pete, I thank you *for the company* for personally helping the *company* out! I knew the *company* could count on you as usual."

There are several issues to recognize in acknowledging people. First, when you express a *company* "thank you," you're promoting their experience and expression of commitment to the company. Second, you're able to use The Change Triangle to ask them to step out of character to behave in a way that you can't evoke on a personal basis.

Finally, when you acknowledge a person for a job well done, consider what you want to promote. What do you most appreciate in the job performance: the person's individual talents or the person's commitment to the company? Often managers thank someone for being good at the specific job or for a personal attribute such as perseverance or taking care of the customer. While that's important and promotes individual excellence, it overlooks the Managing By Influence leverage of company commitment. Rather than focus on the specific job, try this: "Of course the company appreciates how well you did that, but I really thank you for the way your extraordinary effort reflects your great commitment to the company." Focus on taking care of the company and being committed to the company.

When you thank someone for anything, just add:

—The company thanks you.

—As president (or a manager) of this company, I thank you.

—Thanks for a good company job. I always count on that from you. That's what makes you so easy to work with.

You have many opportunities to thank people everyday. See what you're promoting. Watch with Beginner's Mind to see how many acknowledgment opportunities you miss. How many times do you promote personal loyalties? How often do you take the commitment for granted? You're the boss— where are you taking your company?

## 5. Schedule Commitment Meetings

Hold meetings to promote commitment to the company. This will evoke an expression of commitment in many ways. The fact that you would take company time to address the issue will let people know it's a high priority with you.

If your group is small, include everyone. If your group is large, have initial meetings with your immediate staff to get their ideas and their support for involving others. Then gather people from across categories for more commitment meetings. For example, include new and old employees, managers and workers, and people from different departments.

Tell people your purpose is to foster mutual commitment among all workers, the company, and yourself. Explain your ideas and share your feelings about commitment and the company. Step out of character to show your vulnerable side if you haven't normally done this. Tell them you need their help, and you know you can count on them since they care about the company too. In your early meetings, be sure to gather people who have shown you their commitment; then you'll be able to communicate openly and directly without too much effort. As the climate spreads through the company, you'll be able to talk like this to more and more people.

Have them rate the present level of commitment: (a) of the people to the company and, (b) of the company to the people. Score it from 0 to 10. Have them determine what scores they think are needed: (c) for the people to be able to count on their company, and (d) for the company to be able to count on its people. Collect the scores and see how ratings (a) and (b) compare to (c) and (d). Acknowledge the results. Ask how you and the company can improve the situation, making it even better or bringing it up to standard.

Try asking these questions:

- –How can the company better express its commitment to you?
- –How can you better express your commitment to the company?
- –If you know an employee isn't committed to the company, do you treat him or her differently than one you know is committed? If so, how?
- –How is commitment important to you in your work at our company?
- –What are you willing to do to bring out commitment in the people you work with?

As in much of management, the process is the product itself. These commitment meetings will help you focus yourself and raise your consciousness on commitment. They will become a mirror for you to see how well you are promoting the climate of commitment. The process of the meetings will also create several climates very useful to your purposes: *The boss cares about commitment and about the people; We all contribute to commitment, and it's everybody's business; It's okay to express your commitment here;* and *Everyone's opinion is valued.* These messages will return to the workplace, creating Managing By Influence leverage. When you hear the staff's suggestions, let them know what they can expect from you. After you do these things, reconvene to give a report to them and hear reports from them on their actions.

## 6. Start New Employees With a Lesson on Commitment

When do you start discussing commitment with a new employee? At the beginning, of course. As soon as the new person reports to you, meet with him or her to set a climate for success. Have it marked on your calendar with adequate time to discuss all the important issues that will build an effective relationship. Show new people they are a high priority with you.

Begin by establishing the rapport. "Bill, I'd like to tell you that you don't need to make believe you know all about your job today. We know you know less about your job today than any day you'll be on the job. So we welcome you, and I want to tell you the most important information you'll need to be successful here. You're already a member of our team. You don't have to get to know us before you can feel free to count on us. We assume the best of you. We're glad you're on our team; that's all that's important. You can't prove yourself in one day; it will take time, so just relax. We're with you. We're on your side, and we recognize you're on our side." By doing this, you're not only saying the words, but also demonstrating rapport. People talk to someone in this way only when they have rapport.

Often new people will not fully comprehend you because it's hard to absorb everything on the first day. Some new people have only worked in a climate of *Taking care of number one.* You can help their experience of the climate of company commitment by arranging for new people to meet and lunch with others on your staff. They can back up what you've said. If you've established a strong company relationship with your people, you can ask them to help you get the message across to a new person. Their words will have great impact.

## 7. Express the Company's Commitment

For people to be able to express their commitment to a company, they have to sense the commitment the company has to them. Effective leadership therefore requires a climate of expressed commitment from the company to the people.

How does a company express its commitment to its people? Through the rate of pay, the working conditions, the signs of appreciation, and the verbal expressions from leadership. There are other positive acts such as promoting from within, paying for training, encouraging career paths within the company, and recognition and benefits for longevity.

But most people don't trust commitments until they are tested. Human nature teaches us to look at the "down side" of the situation. Anyone can be happy when things are going well, but what happens if . . . ? And usually, the down side is not openly discussed in a positive way. Just as no one can have a 100 percent commitment, no company can have a 100 percent commitment to its people. However, if the company has a deteriorating relationship with one of its people or severs relations, it can still do so in a way that expresses its commitment to the person.

A good performance review process shows the company's commitment to its people. You can make this statement: "We have a commitment to you that you'll be reviewed periodically (at least quarterly) for performance and promotion. If your work ever becomes substandard, jeopardizing your position, we'll put you on probation. Because we are committed to you, we're willing to work with you through a probationary period with weekly reviews. The probation is designed for you to be successful and get off probation. We're willing to train you and tell you the truth about whether you're doing a good job or not. You won't be surprised by us. If you're not on probation, your work is at least satisfactory, and you should not worry about your position with the company.

"If you do not work yourself off probation in six weeks, your employment will be severed. We will pay you three weeks' severance settlement, and thank you for your efforts. If you decide not to go on probation but to resign, upon one week's notice and successful transfer of your duties to another person, we will pay three weeks severance settlement and thank you for your efforts. The only way your employment can be severed without probation is for extreme reasons such as theft."

Now that you've spelled out the worst case, assuring people they won't be surprised and that they will have a safety net, your people can relax and reciprocate the commitment.

When someone is terminated, many companies go "underground" with the facts. Often people are let go because they won't work in a company way, won't step out of character, or won't fit in. Sometimes these people resign, often under pressure. In these cases, the climate can be forwarded by making the facts known. If you let people think the person is gone because of poor skills when it was really an attitude, you're giving the wrong message. The people left behind normally know the truth about how difficult it was to work with the ex-employee, so you have a chance to forward the spirit of common commitment. You might say, "I don't want to talk about Fred now that he's gone, but I do want to set the record straight for the benefit of the company and the rest of us who are still here. Fred's work was substandard in that he wasn't able to work for the good of the company. His skills were not the issue. If Fred had not resigned, we would have had to take action since his behavior created a bad situation and climate for the rest of us." The purpose is not to criticize Fred, but to confirm the priorities and climate.

The company's commitment has a *yes* and a *but,* just like all of life. If you avoid the issue, the fear of the unknown will make it a *yes but* experience and rob from people's ability to experience and express their commitment to the company. Present it in a *but yes* way so it contributes to the harmony and commitment of the workplace.

---

A manager resigned from a bank in Portland. Traditionally, managers there gave three weeks' notice, but he gave only two. During the first week of his notice period, he missed three days. His boss called the Human Resources department and said, "I want to terminate this guy now and tell him we don't need the rest of his notice—tell him not to come in any more and stop paying him." The vice-president of Human Resources said, "No. Tell him not to come in anymore, but pay him for the rest of the two weeks. We have a commitment to all of our people regardless of the actions of one employee. We have to take care of him in a way that makes the rest of our people feel at ease. When we give our word, we keep it—no matter what!" That's one way this particular company expressed its commitment to its people, by saying, in effect, "Even in severance, we'll live up to our commitment to you."

### 8. Send Letters Home

When someone has demonstrated commitment to the company in a noteworthy way, write the person a letter of acknowledgment and mail it to his or her home. This gives the person a chance to feel good about the company with his or her family. You can include an expression of appreciation to the family for the support it gives the employee. This also serves to eliminate the home as a haven for bellyaching about the job, because it gives the employee and the family a chance to acknowledge to each other that the company is a good place to work.

When looking for reasons to write, don't wait for something earthshaking, only noteworthy; for example, excellent attendance, long hours on a project, or consistently good results. Any reason can be a good one. In signing the letter, have your company title typed in but make your handwritten signature as informal as you feel easy with. This blends the company relationship with your personal appreciation.

## 9. Kill Gossip But Promote Informal Communication

Gossip is personal or intimate news and it spreads for personal reasons. It meets no standard of service to the company, being conveyed on an interpersonal basis rather than intraorganizational. Gossip is normally counterproductive in an organization because it lacks accountability. Its personal nature interferes with the climate of commitment to the organization. On the other hand, every organization needs informal communication since no formal communication system can ever get the full job done. Informal communication differs from gossip in that it exists for the good of the company and must meet that standard.

You can promote informal communication and kill gossip several ways. Let people know how you feel about gossip and tell them you are committed to open communication. Advise them to come to you whenever they hear information that they want verified. When they come to you, be truthful. Give them facts; tell them you don't know if you don't; or tell them the information isn't public now but will be made available as soon as it's in the company's interest. Let them know you'll get the word out quickly; they won't have to dig it out.

Be sure to feed information into the informal network and tell people to spread it around, using you as the source. Make a point of getting information out quickly. Work with your staff to be more conscious of getting company information disseminated without workers having to ask. Create a climate of sharing news that honors the mutual care and concern people have for their company. This quality of information promotes the climate *Our company.*

When you hear gossip, ask, "For whose interest are you telling that? How does the company benefit?" Ask the news-bearers to consider the effect the gossip has on the climate of mutual interest. Don't get involved in gossip. When you hear it, tell the people spreading it you're going to take it to the person who is the subject of the gossip, so they had best take it there first. Soon you'll be out of the gossip network if it still exists. Keep yourself in the informal communication network. Ask people if gossip still exists. If it does, use the informal communication lines to let everyone know you're working to stamp it out because it's not in the best interest of the company. This may not be popular, but it works and creates a very productive climate.

## 10. Go Public As Much As Possible

Most of your interactions happen in private with individuals or small groups. While you can accomplish much in this medium, ultimately you'll get maximum leverage by going public.

Get information into the mainstream of the organization by mixing these strategies. For example, you may have sent a letter home to Wendy for outstanding demonstration of commitment. Circulate a copy among top management. Put a copy on the bulletin board with a note, "I wrote this letter to Wendy from all of us." Have her come to an executive committee meeting for an official acknowledgment, and put an item in the company newsletter. Talk it up wherever you go, feeding the grapevine. Send a news release to the local papers.

Ask your people to report instances of company commitment to you, then go to those people to acknowledge them at their workplace. Talk loudly in the hallways to get your message out. If someone says you're making an awfully big deal about it, tell him he's right—it *is* an awfully big deal to you.

## BE ACTIVE IN BUILDING A CLIMATE OF COMMITMENT

Is this more than you feel comfortable with? If so, step out of character for the good of your company, because you're committed. If you pass up these chances, taking the commitment for granted, you're still using leverage, only in a different direction. When you consider the benefits of expressed commitment and the costs of noncommitment, you can't afford not to promote commitment. You have to use every means possible.

You are promoting or deterring the climate of openly expressed commitment in everything you do, 100 times each day. As Giant Food's Izzy Cohen said, "We don't have lip service. What you see is what you get, and what we say is what we do. There are no magic formulas, no secret recipes in our business. It's attention to basics, and we try to instill the Golden Rule in everyone: You treat everyone the way you'd like to be treated. Like any other business, there's no instant success and no instant failure."

Treat your people fairly, not playing personal favorites. Focus on and assume commitment in each employee until you satisfy yourself that you've done everything possible to bring it out. Then, if you can't find any in a particular employee and you've discussed it with the person, let him or her go so you don't honor and promote "lack of commitment." Go public about why you did this, letting people know the person was treated fairly, with a chance to change. Be sure other employees know there was adequate notice and severance. Ask The Question of Influence to learn how you could have done better. Ask your people for their ideas. By your actions, you will have created the climate.

The bad news is: The buck stops here. The good news is: The buck starts here! It's the same news with a different focus, and that depends on your point of view. Take the useful point of view: it's all under your control now. Make the most of the situation. Effective leading begins by taking conscious responsibility for the influence you already have.

## HOW THE ROUSE COMPANY USES COMMITMENT IN MATRIX MANAGEMENT

Recognizing the importance of common commitment in matrix management, and limited by the lack of time or opportunity to provide direct management, Bruce Alexander looks to the more subtle means of leadership.

He says, "I try very hard to separate business discussions from personal interactions. I go out of my way to say hello to people when I see them, and to use their names. I want them to know they can count on me not to let my concerns about business issues carry over into a personal discussion. I'll go out of my way after a meeting to say something on a personal level to the individual with whom I just had a tough exchange on a business point, as a signal that there's nothing personal." Just differentiating between the two relationships, personal and business, will enhance the quality of the business relationship.

In implementing a management by objectives system, where each person agrees on specific performance objectives, Alexander found benefits not fully expected. He explains, "Management by objectives has made an important impact on the company. It's not just in the compensation area, although the compensation aspects reinforce the goals, but also in terms of communicating to each member of the team a set of mutual goals and having these goals shared by everyone. The process of setting the objectives has been enormously important.

"When we started management by objectives, I was astonished to listen to the people from the various matrix disciplines—leasing, marketing, design, construction—and hear how their views of the goals and objectives for the project differed. Even in the most basic, objective areas of budget and schedule, there were differences. People were not communicating. Now we're expanding the use of team objectives for more disciplines to get an entire project team, regardless of which department or division they come from, agreeing on common team objectives and goals, not just their department goals."

Alexander has been pressing development directors to do a better job of communicating the basis and rationale of their decisions. While it adds to the already overwhelming demands on their time, the cost of lack of communication is too great. He says, "When they don't communicate well enough, their decisions are seen as whimsical, capricious, or self-interested when in fact 95 percent of the time they're based on what's good for the project. However, it just hasn't been communicated in a way the whole team understands. Once this climate of distrust and self-interest is born, the project has an uphill struggle to make it. The survival of our company depends on everyone working together to make our projects successful.

"If management by objectives did nothing other than provide for common understanding of common and individual goals, thereby breeding mutual commitment and trust, it would be worth the effort. That's the real leverage of it.

"I see many companies with a tendency, in an effort to become efficient, to build walls around departments. It seems easier to do this because communication takes time. A lot of managers take the view that they don't have time to communicate, so you have a lot of pieces of some companies operating in their own fiefdoms with their own separate understandings of what should be common goals."

Alexander talks about the use of purpose at The Rouse Company. "One of the things that makes our people so good is the mission of the company. It's important that we have a return for our shareholders, but the company has always felt there were two additional critical elements of the company's goals: first, to fulfill the capabilities of our employees, and second, to improve the quality of life in America. And the fact that we're working on such a vital issue, improving the quality of life in America, makes people feel that they do important and legitimate work. And from that mission comes great motivation for what we do.

"I can make demands of people knowing that they're committed to something really important. Let me tell you—I have to go around here on Friday nights and literally force people to go home. I'm here at 6 or 6:15, and there'll be a cadre of people here working, and I have to go to them and say,

'You've worked enough this week, it's time to go home. Go home and be with your family.' How many bosses have to ask people to leave the office at 6 o'clock on Friday night?"

Finally, Bruce Alexander talks about dealing directly and sensitively with the matter of an individual's commitment. "Everyone comes to a point, for many about age forty, where they question whether they want to continue to commit themselves to a company. And I think that for a number of people that I've had as senior managers, it's been critical, in terms of their effectiveness in operating, to challenge them to determine if they wanted to continue to commit themselves to the company or not. This has been enormously useful in resolving some issues in their mind and making them much more effective people.

"It's also not easy to ask because they might say no. But I feel it's much better to have them say no and deal with that than to deal with an uncertain commitment over the next five or ten years. Because I find that many of these things just drag on and on and on. People don't resolve them unless you force them to resolve them.

"I learn of their uncertainty in different ways. It may be other job offers. It may be in conversation where they express that they think they want to do something else. It may be a state of mind that makes them not particularly pleasant to deal with, just in terms of interpersonal relations with other people in the company, because they're not sure they really want to be doing what they're doing. And I just put all that out on the table.

"I tell them, 'I want to have this conversation in a non-threatening way. I think you're uncertain about your career. And I want to lay out some alternatives for you. If you want to do something else, I'll help you get situated.' In some cases, I've offered to give people consulting contracts so they could phase out over a gradual period of time and not worry about financial concerns. But I say to them, 'In a certain period of time, I want you to decide if you really want to be here, or if you really want to do something else. And for your own good and the good of the company, you've got to make that decision, make the commitment; not forever, but so you can do your day-to-day work in a responsible way for the immediate future.' Then I can relate to them in a way that's appropriate to their commitment."

Bruce Alexander is a very busy man. Starting three projects every year is like starting three new companies every year. He doesn't have time to waste on useless or frivolous management activities. He devotes energies to nurturing commitment because it's time- and cost-effective in getting The Rouse Company's job done.

## HOW THE GIANT FOOD "FAMILY" EXPRESSES COMMITMENT

To Izzy Cohen, Giant Food is more than just a family business, it's a family in itself. He treats his associates at Giant as he would his family. For example, he says, "We never take an adversarial position at the bargaining table, and we try to be fair. We try to negotiate as hard as we can, but I don't remember having any kind of labor problems in the past ten to fifteen years. We get along very well with the labor representatives and naturally with our people. But we're not nice to our people just at negotiating time or thirty days before negotiating time; we try to be fair and honest and good and sweet and appreciative 365 days of the year."

Asked about the term "associate," he says, "Years ago, when we put out our newsletter, we called it *We*. We've never identified our people as employees, always as associates, family, organization, or staff—you know, something other than employees. We're very careful to give everyone dignity and pride for what they've done in their association."

Perhaps the relationship between the company and the union best shows the flavor of family. Al Dobbin reveals, "Everyone in our store is in the union except for the store manager. The assistant manager, department manager and all other staffers are union. We're unionized from wall to wall and ceiling to floor. Even though Virginia is a 'right to work' state, I think that 98 percent of our eligible employees are in the union."

Dobbin goes on to explain that one of Giant's biggest challenges is to foster a sense of commitment in unionized employees, so that the unionized employees are "Giant people who are unionized," not "union people who work for Giant." He says, "I think we've been successful at doing that. We've lived with the union for many years. We wouldn't do anything different if we were nonunion.

"We treat our people like our family . . . if the union is there or not there. We have virtually no problem in Giant with grievances. We treat people the way they want to be treated. That's something I harp on, and I say, and I do, and I believe. I think it's so important to maintain the continuity of people, of leadership, as well as of people in the stores. It's not a union/management division. I'm Al Dobbin who started as a part-time checker. I don't feel differently (maybe a little older) than when I started."

In keeping with the concept of "family," Giant likes to hire people who actually are related. In a beautiful publication titled *Annual Associates Report,* the company boasts of the families who work at Giant. The cover statement from Izzy Cohen says, "Ours is a family. We need only to look around to see that we have second and third generations beginning to take their place in our organization. We are working for our security—and theirs." Inside the report he credits the associates for the company's success. As he congratulates them for sales and earnings, he refers to "the spirit that has sustained us and will continue to give us a bright, rewarding future for all members of our Giant Family." Cohen tells associates, every time he has an opportunity, that second and third generations are welcome to come to work for the company.

To avoid nepotism, none of the principals' families are involved except as board members. Says Dobbin, "We are a very professionally managed company. We're not a Mom-and-Pop kind of store, or a family-run business anymore. The kids know they're in competition with everyone else.

"We work hard to maintain what we've got. That is the secret to our success . . . our people, the people who have grown up in the business, the second generation that understands what we're all about. We are informal and people oriented. We do anything we can to help our people. There are countless stories of people who've had tragedy in the family and what the company has done to help them. If we ever lost this relationship, this family feeling, Giant wouldn't be Giant, and I wouldn't want to be here. It's important, it's a way of life for us.

"It takes a lot of work. It takes our getting around and walking into an office and saying hi. When I ran distribution, I still tried to get into the warehouses and say hello to the guys on the floors, and let them know we're real people. And I'm constantly pushing my people to do the same."

Finally, Al Dobbin points out, "It's not always a bowl of cherries, please understand. But it's the kind of environment, that if you have a problem, if you have diversity, you can turn and get help. We help each other. That's what it means to be a family: we help each other. We're dependent on each other. You can fight within the family, you can have differences, but when there's a need to pull together, we seem to pull together, whether it's in the business or personal family. Giant has displayed that countless times over the years. We have a tremendous loyalty to our people, and our people have a tremendous loyalty to us, to the company. It's a good place to work. In a nutshell, the key to Giant is the people, and the recognition that the people make it happen."

## HOW COMMITMENT LED TO COMMUNICATION IN A TENSE SITUATION

This incident happened to the authors when we were driving home one night. Ken saw red flashing lights behind us. He muttered to Linda, "They'd better not be after me. I've had the cruise control on fifty. They're not going to catch me for speeding."

Then two police cruisers came flying by us. They maneuvered in front of us, filling both lanes and slowing down. "It *is* me they're after!" Ken exclaimed as he pulled off the road. One of the cars dropped behind us and the other stayed in front, blocking our car from moving. It all looked pretty dramatic for a traffic violation.

As soon as we stopped, the officer from the front car came running back and opened Ken's door. He hollered to Ken, "Get out!" The other officer stayed back watching us. Ken was stunned, not even turning off the engine, as the officer continued to yell, "Get out! Get over here!"

Ken got out and walked toward the back of the car where the officer was motioning. The officer shouted, "Put your hands against the car." Ken put his hands against the car while looking at the officer and trying to figure out what was happening. The officer yelled at Ken, "Now move your feet back." Ken, not being accustomed to this type of action, started moving back and the officer angrily shouted, "No, no. Keep your hands on the car and then move your feet back."

Then Ken remembered the way they do things on television, and he leaned over with his hands on the car, his feet back. The police officer, in a very upset voice, full of anguish and concern, said, "How come you pulled up by that lady, slowed down, made her get off the road, got off the road yourself and then pulled up by her again? You were harassing and intimidating her."

Ken had no idea what the officer was talking about. He looked at the officer and said in a calm voice, "Officer, I don't know what you're talking about."

The officer shouted back, still very forcefully, "Well, you were driving on the other side of the road. You kept pulling up next to a lady, and you were frightening her. You drove her off the road. Then you drove off the road. You crossed over the median strip and came back this way."

Ken spoke gently, "Officer, I have no idea what you're talking about, and I've only been on this side of the road." The officer got much calmer and asked, "Well, were you driving on the other side of the road?"

Ken said, "No. Now, may I stand up?" "Yeah, fine," the

officer answered, calming as he talked to Ken. "Look, we had a report from a woman who was being harassed by someone in a car that looks like yours. Do you know anything about that?"

Ken was still very calm and said, "No. I don't know, but I understand you have to assume the worst of me. I've done nothing wrong." The officer nodded. "I guess not, but we need to wait for her to come and identify you." "That's fine," Ken said.

Then the officer walked to the open door of our car. He turned the engine off and said to us, "I want to apologize to you for using force." Ken said, "Fine. I know you were just doing your job." We got to chatting and the officer said, "If I were you I'd probably be very upset." "Well, I'm not," Ken said. "I was brought up to know the police are on my side, and I never had a doubt in my mind that I was quite innocent, and you would take care of me." The woman was brought around and confirmed that it was not our car.

---

That was quite a lesson in communication. If you don't have rapport, you don't have communication. Rapport means a relationship marked with harmony, accord, and affinity. If you have a relationship marked with disharmony, you don't have communication. People will go out of their way to *not* communicate with others if they feel out of harmony. Rapport depends on trust. If you don't have trust, you have a relationship marked with distrust. Trust depends on commitment. When you determine whom to trust, you ask yourself, "What is this person committed to?" You don't just listen to what someone says; a part of you is asking, "Why is he or she saying that? What's her motivation? Whose bread is she buttering?" Or: "What's he up to? Where's he coming from?"

Communication is the deep exchange of experience that brings the two parties to a full understanding of each other, including the understanding that they understand each other. The officer didn't communicate with Ken. He didn't want to let Ken know of his own fear. He covered that by bravado, doing his best to look in control of a situation that he feared could be out of control. If Ken was the person who had done what the woman had said, then Ken was only committed to his own personal agenda in life, regardless of the human cost. The officer assumed that Ken was dangerous, ready to do him harm at any moment. He'd be a fool to assume anything else as he started into that relationship.

Ken, on the other hand, started with a trusting relationship, accepting that the police are committed to the public good. He had been raised on that notion. Ken could be fully open, sharing his innocence and his lack of savvy in this type of situation. He had nothing to hide, no need to posture any particular way, knowing that everything would work out all right. Ken's entire demeanor communicated this common ground with the officer. It took only moments for the officer to pick it up. Had Ken felt he needed to protect himself, he might have acted with some bravado of his own, which could have escalated the situation and put it on a dangerous spiral of two people reacting to each other—more like billiard balls banging into each other on a pool table than like human beings. It didn't take two to build communication, just one who was satisfied with the commitment of the other.

## MBI ACTIONS

**#49.** Think of the extent to which you foster personal commitment and behavior from your people. What are the benefits of doing this? What are the costs? In a situation where the costs now outweigh the benefits, use The Question of Influence to learn how you made it happen and take a new approach in order to change it.

**#50.** Try the ten strategies discussed in this chapter on whatever level you feel appropriate. Better yet, go a little beyond what seemed appropriate in the past. As you apply them, monitor your organization, looking for benefits in communication, cooperation, innovation, conflict resolution, problem solution, and a general sense of responsibility from the rest of the people in your organization.

# 8

# Achieving MBI

Leadership is the total effect you have on the people and events around you. This total effect is your influence. Effective leading is being consciously responsible for your organizational influence.

As you've read and thought about how you influence your organization, you have already begun unconsciously applying your discoveries, just like athletes who see themselves on replays. If you've worked through the MBI ACTIONS, you have also been consciously applying your new knowledge as you've progressed through the steps of the total concept. Now that you've seen the whole, it's time to get down to serious work implementing your plans for your organization, using your renewed potency to lead.

Regardless of what you have applied from *Managing By Influence* and how effectively you've led your organization in the past, this chapter is designed to assist you in making major new strides and building support systems which will keep you moving ahead. Remember the premise: You're either moving ahead or you're falling behind—there is no hovering in the status quo. Whenever you need a refresher, come back to this chapter.

## THE LEVERAGE OF MANAGING BY INFLUENCE

Leverage is gained by finding out how to make your small acts produce large results. Picture yourself grabbing the short end of a lever to make the other end move in big

ways. You can do this only if you recognize your power. There-
in lies the irony: the little things you do *already* have big
effects. When you are the boss, you can never not lead.
Whether you realize it or not, you're always in control. To
gain power, recognize it and use it. Take this point of view for
two reasons. First, it's the truth (and it's always best to go
with the truth). Second, it's the only useful point of view
(even at those times when you doubt it's the truth). Use The
Question of Influence as a mirror. Ask: "What did I do (or not
do) to make this happen (or not happen)?" If you can't find the
answer by yourself, ask the people around you.

If you come away with nothing more from this book, keep
this phrase in your head: YOU CAN NEVER NOT LEAD. If
you gain only one technique, make it the use of The Question
of Influence. Ask it when things go badly and when things go
well. Put it on your checklist for every meeting, every project,
every moment. If you use it in your private life, it will give
you new insight and power there as well.

### Lever 1: Leading to Change

The major block to leading to change is the attitude that
things won't change—the past determines the future. To
some extent, everyone's thought process includes this point of
view. Using the words of the first technique of The Change
Triangle—"in the past"—help yourself and others break this
pattern and create a new potential. Add "in the past" to your
thoughts and your conversations. Then use the second technique, asking people to "step out of character," to make major
changes. When asking people to go beyond their "personalities," into their "companalities," call on their commitment
using the third technique, the power base, of The Change
Triangle—"for the good of the company." This will give them
abilities they don't normally use in their private lives. As a
side benefit, this self-discovery will enhance their private
lives.

If you think your people are not open to change, look for
the source of the matter by remembering the full extent of

your influence. Start with your own behavior and step out of character for the good of your company. Even if someone hasn't shown you that he or she cares enough to be called on this way, it's your job to go first. Take the risk of looking foolish. Step out of character and lead the way. Whether you succeed or fail, ask The Question of Influence so you'll learn from the situation. You can't be sure you can't do it until you try; but you can be sure matters will stay the same if you don't try.

**Lever 2: Managing the Climate**

To avoid drowning in details, you must employ some form of management by exception, delegating authority to others. However, to be responsible as a manager, you need some way to influence the management of the details you've delegated. You can accomplish this Managing By Influence leverage by managing the climate. There's always a climate whether you recognize it or not. And it always affects all the people and events of the company, just as the atmosphere affects all of life. As the boss, you always affect the climate. While many managers try to recognize their impact on any given interaction, they seldom consider the influence that one instance has on the climate. The Question of Influence will serve to find your effect on the climate.

Often managers do their best under the circumstances, rather than set out to create a climate which is favorable to the company. By allowing the existing climate to continue, you are giving it tacit approval. To break this cycle, monitor the climate both on a routine basis and in times of exceptional success or failure. Once the climate is identified, there are strategies for reinforcing or changing it. To be more effective in leadership, use Climate Check as a monitoring technique and follow with The Question of Influence. Encourage your people to do Climate Checks by asking them for their reading of the climate at meetings and in normal business conversations. Lead people to a more powerful outlook on the part they each play in the organization by realizing the impact they have on the climate. Create a climate of responsibility for the climate.

## Lever 3: Promoting Commitment

The driving force of any organization is the commitment of its people. People want to be committed and express their commitment, but leadership often tolerates a climate which impedes this expression. A vicious cycle develops when people conceal their commitment until it's safe to show it, and managers don't call on people to act committed because they haven't shown commitment in the past. This vicious cycle leaves people unsatisfied and companies unable to compete.

Since the game is called "Follow the Leader," it's your job to go first. Understanding that no one is 100 percent committed to anything, focus on the part of people that is committed and you'll call that forth. Assume the commitment exists, ready to be expressed at the appropriate time. It's the useful point of view. When you evoke an expression of commitment from your people, you create the basis of problem solution, conflict resolution, and open, honest company communication. Commitment is the cure for "protect your turf" and cynicism, two behaviors that harm organizations. Remembering that you're always using influence, see what you're promoting now. Ask The Question of Influence to learn how your little acts affect your organization through your leverage. No single result bears more reward than the development of the experience and expression of common commitment to the organization. It's worth your time and effort; and if you don't give it your time and effort, you're saying something, too.

## HOW TO TIE IT ALL TOGETHER

Tie Managing By Influence together. Create a climate of commitment to the organization. Use the climate to call on people to step out of character. Ask people to look beyond their own jobs to see how they affect the climate of their department or the whole company. Ask them to recognize how the little things they do give them leverage in their work area. Promote this climate of commitment to new employees. Reinforce the experience in older employees who have come to take it for granted. Create a climate of stepping out of character which will sweep people off their feet and make your organization the most exciting part of their lives. Let them take their new enthusiasm home and get encouragement from their friends and family about the great place they work. Use all these strategies to share the leadership of your organization with all your people.

## A CHALLENGE IN APPLICATION

When a boy starts off to fish using grasshoppers as bait, he collects them in a big jar. He finds the first one, throws it in the jar and puts the lid back on, looking for another one. As he walks, he hears "ping, ping"—that's the grasshopper jumping up and hitting its head on the lid. When he finds another one, he quickly sneaks it in, not letting the first one jump out. Now he hears "ping, ping, ping, ping." After putting about a dozen grasshoppers in this jar, all going "ping, ping, ping, ping, ping, ping, ping," he hikes to his fishing spot.

When he arrives there, he puts the jar down. But now the jar is very quiet. All the grasshoppers are sitting on the bottom. He opens the jar and takes out a grasshopper and doesn't bother to put the lid back on. The grasshoppers have stopped jumping. Apparently, they've figured out that every time they jump up they get a loud noise, a headache, and wind up back on the bottom real fast. So to save themselves the trouble, they just stay there, prepared to spend the rest of their lives in the jar.

The grasshoppers have put a limitation on their little grasshopper selves that was valid at one point (because they had hit their heads), but now is no longer appropriate. The same thing occurs with people. They make decisions that may be very accurate and very valuable at one point, but may not be true the next day. You too have your self-imposed leadership limitations, since being a manager is sometimes like being a grasshopper—you occasionally go out to get the job done and wind up, with a loud ping and a headache, back where you started. You now have a growth opportunity to see where you've made grasshopper decisions in the past. While they may have been appropriate then, the lid may now be off.

In taking on the challenge of applying Managing By Influence, consider that each new moment has a new potential. And even if you try without success today, tomorrow brings a new opportunity. If this hasn't been typical for you in the past, use your improved ability to step out of character.

## PLANNING FOR MANAGING BY INFLUENCE

Like any part of your management, application of your full leadership ability will take planning. If you see that the results of more effective leadership and the application of Managing By Influence leverage will be useful to you and your organization, apply yourself to the task of implementation with the same drive and determination that you use for any important company matter. Use the normal planning steps for enhancing your leadership: create a vision, make a strategy, plan your tactics. Follow up with monitoring and close the feedback loop by making adjustments. The Question of Influence will help you with the feedback. You can learn from both your successes and failures.

Don't tackle the biggest problem situation or most difficult person you face on your first outing. Practice your skills on your easier problems and prove to yourself that you have a new beginning. Create a climate of success for yourself. As you succeed at these starting issues, work your way up the scale in degree of difficulty.

Keep your plans up-to-date. You'll probably have quick success and will need to re-challenge yourself. Set aside fifteen minutes on Mondays and Fridays to plan your leadership week and review your results. By making plans you'll be prepared for the spontaneous situations that arise. Chance favors the prepared mind. The benefits of your labor will outweigh the cost of your efforts.

## BE AN ACTIVE LEADER: MAKE IT ALL HAPPEN

The president of a Dallas service company tells of her discovery about active leadership. "When I was a girl, I learned to play tennis. They taught me to await service of the ball by standing on the balls of my feet, racket centered in both hands, and my eye on the ball, poised for action. I did this for many years, until I saw professional tennis on TV.

"Here was a very different approach. The player receiving the serve was jumping around, darting side to side, doing his best to unnerve the server, anticipate the serve direction, and even force the server to put the ball in one area. I saw the difference between being passive and being active. Even though the ball was in the server's court, the receiver assumed he could force the play while waiting.

"I began to recognize these two ways of leading in myself: active and passive. Even when things seemed to be 'in the other person's court,' I could let things happen or make things happen—the choice was mine. I started to ask myself how I could bring work more under my influence and control even when it seemed to be in someone else's court.

"Now I've come to a new realization that there is no such thing as passive leadership. I'm either being actively active or actively passive: both are actions with direct effect since I'm the boss. Recognizing this, I've regained full control of my company. At the same time, I've also been able to give myself more credit for the success we've had, rather than considering it just a matter of good fortune."

## TAKING THE NEXT STEP: TRAINING OTHERS IN MBI

As you accelerate Managing By Influence, people will notice that you're acting somewhat differently. This won't mean you were doing a bad job in the past, but rather that you're engaged in a project of self-development for the good of the company. When people respond to your leadership, you face another opportunity to be active. Start training your people to enhance their innate leadership ability.

Share your process with your people. Tell them about MBI or show them this book. Lead them through by asking them The Question of Influence about their own successes and failures. Ask them to bring you evidence of their discoveries. Schedule meetings with your people to act as a support network for each other as they work through the lessons of the book. When they reach a point of full engagement in the process, have them start training their own people. And so on.

## BRINGING MBI OUT IN OTHERS

Work toward the day when everyone in your organization understands that he or she is a company leader. Your people don't have to *become* leaders, they *already are* leaders. Most people don't recognize their influence on the people and events around them. Imagine a company full of people who know that NO ONE CAN EVER NOT LEAD: think of the immense power.

American business and government leaders have not adequately recognized the leadership of followers in the past. In most cases, the leadership of followers has been: (1) good, due to unconsciously positive leadership; (2) random, due to unconsciously mixed leadership, or (3) bad, due to unconsciously negative leadership. As a result, the leadership of followers has often been squelched.

"Leader" and "follower" are positions in an organization. Leaders require the acceptance of followers. Followers can fire their leaders by going to another organization. While it may be costly to the individual, it's a real possibility at all times. This will be especially apparent if predictions of human resource shortages come true.

Both leaders and followers provide leadership and followership. Leadership and followership are not positions, they are functions of life that everyone performs. Good leadership fosters good followership and good followership fosters good leadership. As executives, managers, and workers recognize their interdependence in the workplace, a "dance" begins with leaders and followers leading and following each other. Recognition emerges that the credit belongs to all.

## HOW TO APPLY MANAGING BY INFLUENCE IN YOUR FAMILY

All these issues of leadership apply to family life as well. Most parents don't recognize the full extent of the influence they have on their children, and very few children recognize the full extent of the influence they have on their parents. Furthermore, little of the purpose of the family is fostered. People take commitment to the family as the given nature of things, and then take each other for granted, acting for personal benefit rather than for the good of the family.

Just as in any organization, family members have various commitments, including a commitment in each to his or her own ego. But through thoughtful leadership and using Managing By Influence leverage, a leader (usually a parent) can lead family members to step out of character, create a climate of belonging, and foster a commitment which benefits all without harming anyone. All these strategies can be adapted for home life.

Most executives and managers don't put the priority and effort into the work of their home life that they put into the work of their business life. Have a family meeting and paint a picture of how good it can be. Ask others to share their vision. See where there is mutual commitment. In family life as in management, the process is often the product.

## FIND YOUR OWN EFFECTIVE LEADERSHIP STYLE

There is no one style that works best for everybody. Every style can be successful when applied with The Question of Influence.

Make a list of the various ways you *force* people to achieve results and a list of how you *influence* people to achieve results. Then look at the results you've created each way and compare these results to the costs.

For example, one way to force people to results is to nag. Nagging will get the job done many times, and that's a benefit. However, nagging is often costly. It takes a lot of your time and the time of the person you're managing, it doesn't recognize and foster the person's responsibility, and it is unsatisfying to both of you. Furthermore, nagging seldom leads toward less nagging; it perpetuates itself.

In seeing how you influence, consider roles that work well for you, for example: salesperson, promoter, coach, cheerleader, older sister or brother, lead worker, minister, teacher. Particularly focus on situations where you have no authority but get good results.

Refine and use the roles that bring you success in influence, reducing the need to tie yourself up in direct use of force or authority. Put your favorite styles into the context of Managing By Influence to achieve your own individualized leadership style. It's in you already—recognize it and let it out, for the good of your organization.

### THE VALUE OF BELONGING TO AN ORGANIZATION

There's deep value in belonging to organizations. All of us naturally want to belong someplace. The worst feeling in life for a human being is to not belong—to be out of place in life, alone, suffering from separation and alienation. People need to feel part of something.

To achieve this, people become parts of groups. As family life provides less of a feeling of belonging and as people feel less linked to their community, the need to belong can be filled by the place where people work. This is their most conscious place of belonging, a place they come by choice and expend their conscious efforts.

In the past, many organizations said to their people, "Give us your soul each day, and we'll pay you back with a paycheck." It's now time to recognize the new opportunity and truth of the workplace. Organizations that will succeed will say, "Give us your soul each day, and we'll give it back to you with interest, leaving you with more than you brought in. And we'll pay you, too." Organizations can add "interest" to their people's souls by giving them a chance to have dignity, importance, and belonging; and by expressing and demanding commitment (which already exists, anyway), and asking them to step out of character for growth for the good of the company.

Create a climate of partnership with your people—a partnership based on your organization's purpose. And include in the purpose the need to provide a place of belonging, purpose, and growth for your people.

When you achieve this, the people will nurture the organization and work with common interest as a body of leaders. Notice that your hands don't complain about taking care of your feet, and your feet don't complain that the head never carries the body. All these parts have their own function within the larger body. The same thing is possible for the body of your organization.

## LEARNING BY DISCOVERY

When you make a discovery like Managing By Influence, it's not like learning that debits go on the left or there are five steps in a planning cycle—it's not that type of information. It's the type of information that is like learning to ride a bicycle.

When you go from not being a bike rider to being a bike rider, it's not something you forget. People who haven't ridden a bike for ten years can still ride. People who haven't been swimming in a long time don't get in and say, "I wonder if I can still swim." It's not something you need to remember—it's an experience.

When a grasshopper realizes the lid's off, it doesn't stop and say, "Well, what's the significance of the lid being off?" Rather, its whole way of looking at things is altered and it

knows how to act. When you discover something new, everything changes.

It's like falling in love. Imagine a woman who knows a
man who is sometimes wonderful and sometimes creepy.
When she falls in love with him, suddenly the wonderful
things are wonderful and the creepy things are wonderful—
everything's wonderful. If she falls out of love, the wonderful
things are creepy and the creepy things are creepy. Her entire
point of view alters, and her experience changes with it.

In discovering the full extent of your influence, you'll see
powers you have that you may have forgotten or never
noticed. Everything will be different with the new point of
view you've discovered. (You may be re-discovering it—life is
a never-ending process of re-discovery.) Go back to the special
laboratory called "work" to try your stuff. Then step back and
see how it worked, and try some more. You can't lose with
active leadership and your efforts to grow.

## ARE YOU EASILY DISCOURAGED?

From time to time, life as a leader can look hopeless.
After taking a hard look in the mirror at your leadership, you
may be overwhelmed by the focus on what's needed. To help
you, consider a man who lived through this:

> Failed in business in '31
>
> Defeated for the Legislature in '32
>
> Again failed in business in '34
>
> Sweetheart died in '35
>
> Had a nervous breakdown in '36
>
> Defeated in election in '38
>
> Defeated for Congress in '43
>
> Defeated for Congress in '46
>
> Defeated for Congress in '48
>
> Defeated for Senate in '55

Defeated for Vice-President in '56
Defeated for Senate in '58
Elected President in '60

This man was Abraham Lincoln.

# Afterword

The purpose of Schatz and Company is to contribute a technology that enables organizations to fulfill their purpose. Two years ago, we confronted our purpose statement and the need to disseminate this technology on a larger scale. If this was truly our purpose, more was needed. Since we chose not to expand or franchise, we decided to write this book. During all the times of discouragement, when perseverance was called for in extraordinary amounts, we returned to our purpose statement. It renewed our commitment and determination.

Upon your completion of *Managing By Influence*—Congratulations! Our ultimate reward is the use you make of the book. Since writing a book is a one-way communication, we appreciate feedback and encourage any comments or sharing of the ways you've been able to apply the lessons of this book. Please write to us at P.O. Box 22874, Alexandria, VA 22304.

Should you want direct support from us in implementing MBI in your own organization, call us regarding our Managing By Influence™ seminar and speeches. You can reach us at Schatz and Company, (703) 370-7110.

# APPENDIX **1**

# A Self-Appraisal

—*Leadership* is the total effect you have on the people and events around you.

—This total effect is your *influence*.

—Effective leading is being consciously responsible for your *organizational influence*.

---

Score your answer to each question and add your total. Notice that Group 2 questions have reversed scoring.

*Group 1 Questions*

| Almost | | | | Almost | |
|---|---|---|---|---|---|
| Always / | Always / | Often / | Seldom / | Never / | Never |
| 1 | 2 | 3 | 4 | 5 | 6 |

**1 2 3 4 5 6**   I feel my responsibility is greater than my influence.

**1 2 3 4 5 6**   I feel things are out of my control.

**1 2 3 4 5 6**   I think: If I had my way, things would be different around here.

**1 2 3 4 5 6**   I find that I just can't get people to do things the way I'd like them to be done.

**1 2 3 4 5 6**   I get things done primarily because of my authority, not my influence.

**1 2 3 4 5 6**   I think: I wonder why he doesn't do what I want; I've told him three times already.

**1 2 3 4 5 6**   If I get the sense that one of my people will not carry out an assignment the way I want it done, I just talk more loudly and firmly.

**1 2 3 4 5 6**   I give assignments, let the chips fall where they may, and then hope for the best.

**1 2 3 4 5 6**   I use management techniques that worked for me once but may no longer be effective.

**1 2 3 4 5 6**   I have abandoned good ideas in the past because I couldn't get them implemented.

**1 2 3 4 5 6**   I put up with situations I've been trying to change but can't.

**1 2 3 4 5 6**   I look the other way on difficult occasions because I don't think I can improve them.

**1 2 3 4 5 6**   I find my organization's climate is not what I'd like it to be.

**1 2 3 4 5 6**   I feel lonely and burdened in my job.

**1 2 3 4 5 6**   I am cynical about my employees.

**1 2 3 4 5 6**   I think my employees are cynical.

**1 2 3 4 5 6**   I base working relations on strong personal loyalties from my people.

**1 2 3 4 5 6**   I have trouble getting people to work together.

**1 2 3 4 5 6**   I have difficulty resolving conflicts between my people.

**1 2 3 4 5 6**   I avoid confronting conflicts even if they are hurting the organization.

*Group 2 Questions*

|  | Almost |  |  | Almost |  |
|---|---|---|---|---|---|
| Always / | Always / | Often / | Seldom / | Never / | Never |
| 6 | 5 | 4 | 3 | 2 | 1 |

**6 5 4 3 2 1**   I can lead resistant people to change.

**6 5 4 3 2 1**   I am willing to step out of character if it's needed to get the job done.

6 5 4 3 2 1     I am aware of the climate of my organization.

6 5 4 3 2 1     I recognize my effect on the climate.

6 5 4 3 2 1     I routinely take time to plan or manage the climate.

6 5 4 3 2 1     If I notice the climate is wrong, I make it right.

6 5 4 3 2 1     I know how to effectively create a climate for my organization.

6 5 4 3 2 1     I know how to facilitate open, direct communication.

6 5 4 3 2 1     I know how to bring out commitment to my organization.

6 5 4 3 2 1     I treat my people as if they are committed to my organization even if they haven't expressed it verbally.

Score your answer to each question and add your total. Notice that Group 2 questions have reversed scoring.

**Rate yourself:**

**151–180:**    Very high awareness of my organizational influence.

**121–150:**    High awareness of my organizational influence.

**91–120:**    Moderate awareness of my organizational influence.

**Below 91:**    Low awareness of my organizational influence.

# A Study in Managing By Influence: Giant Food's "Company's Coming"

Giant Food's annual program called "Company's Coming," in which top management visits every single store and facility, uses much of the technology and many of the strategies of Managing By Influence. It's had extraordinary success in providing management leverage for Giant's executives. The program is presented here as a case study of principles, but it can also be adapted to your organization, large or small.

### A Campaign to Influence 20,000 People

"The original purpose of 'Company's Coming' was to gear up for our busiest time of year, Thanksgiving and Christmas," reports Barry F. Scher, Director of Public Affairs. "Just like you have spring housecleaning, this was our fall housecleaning. Somebody had the idea that it would be good to have a contest—that there was some motivational value to getting people to really pitch in if we offered recognition."

Al Dobbin talks about the informal nature of Giant. "We try to do MBWA. 'Company's Coming' is a perfect example of that. We've been doing this for more than thirty years. We used to do it twice a year when we had fewer stores, now it's once a year.

"When we get into the stores, it's a chance to say hello to friends, to let them know that we care. There's a tremendous amount of togetherness at the store. It's just a tremendous morale-building effort, in addition to getting our stores into what we consider the best condition possible for the holiday season.

"If we can motivate our people to that level during this particular period of time, we can achieve 80 to 90 percent of that the rest of the year. If we can, we'll be better than any other food chain in the country. And I think we do achieve somewhere between 80 to 90 percent of 'Company's Coming' year around. That's part of the secret of our success and our people know it."

Scher says, "It costs us a lot of money in labor to do it, but it's the best investment we can make."

### Purpose and Intended Benefits

"Company's Coming" is still designed to get the stores sparkling clean for the holiday season. Barry Scher tells of other benefits. "It's also designed to rekindle the spirit. It's an opportunity to tell people what we're all about, the philosophy of the company, and a chance to crank everybody up once a year. And you need that. It's a time to appeal to their pride. They're very proud. It's a chance to show you're the best—a chance to put your best foot forward, and get ready for company. And the company's going to be your customer.

"'Company's Coming' is the time the brass comes down out of the ivory tower, and the people see all the vice-presidents. Quite honestly, we don't get around as much as we'd like to. It's a chance to go in and give somebody a pat on the back and say, 'We appreciate what you're doing. Thank you!'

"We get everyone involved. There's input from throughout, and it touches everyone. We reinforce the culture. We all know what it's like to have company, what we do to get ready. That's what we try to do everyday, but once a year we try to do it even more so. We foster pride for accomplishment, and we give recognition. We do our best to let our people know we do in fact care, and we aren't just people who live in an ivory tower. We give our associates a chance to demonstrate just how good they can be. They do some fantastic things."

### Creating a Climate of Success for "Company's Coming"

"Company's Coming" formally begins with a kick-off meeting in August for all managers, supervisors, pharmacy managers, vice-presidents, and directors—500 people. It's held at a country club; the program lasts about two to three hours followed by a picnic and sports.

President Izzy Cohen talks to the group and each vice-president has a chance to speak. Merchandising campaigns, new promotions and plans are introduced. Store managers get the first look at what's new, with management including them in a way befitting the Giant management philosophy. Senior Vice-President of Finance David B Sykes discusses the state of the company with the annual financial report, an insider's preview of his speech for the shareholders' meeting.

At the kick-off meeting, the year's new theme is introduced, such as *The People Who Care; Only the Best; Count on Us.* All managers have a chance to give input. The managers are in on the game. There's nothing being pulled on them. Scher says, "Originally it was that type of surprise inspection, but now, it's *our* game, to get our people cooking."

Each manager gets a manual that details the theme of "Company's Coming." It includes samples of the inspection sheets and rating criteria.

Says Al Dobbin, "I love to tell them, 'I know that angels don't come in and put the groceries on your shelves, and I know that they don't scrub your floor, but it gets done.' So I thank them. And that sets the spirit of 'Company's Coming' for me."

### Planning and Execution

All 144 stores are inspected in September and October. Factories, warehouses, and truck drivers have their own form of "Company's Coming." Each store is visited on one day by all management from vice-presidents up as well as by an inspection team made up of zone and department managers from other areas. These people arrive at various times during the day. Anywhere from four to twelve stores will be visited in a single day. Each visiting group will walk with the manager and make a point of seeing each of the department heads and as many people as possible.

Barry Scher explains, "It used to be, way back in the dark ages, that it was a surprise. In fact, they didn't even tell them the day, and 'Company's Coming' lasted for two months—but that was impractical. So we started publishing the schedule in the middle of the summer, and said this is when you've got to get yourself ready. They will know by the day before in what order the stores will be visited."

The district manager, who is the team leader, has two sets of rating sheets, one that the team uses to rate and one to give to the department manager in the store. Each of them rates their own department. It doesn't have any bearing on the official rating but it gives them an opportunity to rate themselves.

Each rating team is chaired by a district manager from a different district. The stores compete only within their own district so there's no favoritism. Teams do not rate their own stores. Each district manager takes his produce, deli, and meat supervisors. They're the raters. In addition, there are pharmacy raters and bakery specialists. The raters are the official company standard-bearers.

Three entire issues of *We,* the Giant internal newsmagazine, are devoted to "Company's Coming," with pictures of the people—not just the award stores, but every store. There are recognition banquets for the winners. There are plaques for the best stores in each zone and for departments, too. It's a chance to give recognition. Winning stores and departments get patches to wear on their sleeves.

## How Different Stores Respond

Scher reports, "Some stores run their own mini-campaigns, with buttons and souvenirs they give to the visitors.

They'll get pens printed up with 'Store 19 welcomes you to Company's Coming.' They've done all kinds of things. One bakery manager made cookies with the theme written on them. Another time someone who did ceramics made name badges for everyone. Several years ago, since this was getting out of hand, we said, 'Look, the emphasis in "Company's Coming" is on making things right and clean, and you don't have to do a lot of frills in order to win.' So we took away some of that, but some of them still do it because it gives their people a chance to get involved and to come up with something that's theirs. That depends more on the store manager than anything else, but it also depends on the associates and what they can do.

"There's a buzz in the network as one store calls another to see when the different visitors are coming and going. They know where the teams are, the order, and so on. Their desire is to get the rating over with. They d love to be first. Because if they're not first, they've got to keep it going all day. That's when they glare at the customers.

"We have a problem getting people not to work off the clock. It's a violation of our union contract for people to work for no pay. And those of us who go way back know that 'Company's Coming' was the day you worked all night long. It was almost a tradition."

Al Dobbin tells of the effort store managers put forth: "At one time, we used to budget many hours for 'Company's Coming.' We used to set aside extra hours for the stores to get ready. One year, we were in a crunch for profits, and we said, 'We're not going to kill 'Company's Coming,' but we're not going to spend any money for it. It's your job, Mr. Manager. You know what we need. Get it done by better planning, better direction.'

"That year we spent no extra dollars for it. It was only going to be a one-year deal, because that was a year of a crunch. I never really thought we could achieve the level of excellence we achieved. But by saying to our people, this is your problem, guys, we've never returned to the original level of expense for 'Company's Coming.' This was several years ago. Our stores do the job. I ask them each year when I go around how they do it. They say they do it because they plan better, they know that it has to be done and we don't have the money, and 'our pride in this organization makes it happen.' And their people's pride also."

## A View From the Store

Says Store Manager Rennie Coleman, "If you put forth enough effort and happen to win, that effect carries over for the entire year. It's a matter of pride. To see that your store has won an award in a fierce competition . . . well, that means something, that means a lot.

"I think the main benefit I get is the sense of working more together with people. You work together every day you're here and get all the support from everybody, but it's fine-tuned in 'Company's Coming.' It's like putting something together, putting the model together, and going toward the last few pieces. It's like the team arriving, so to speak. It really takes care of a lot of the climate. It's easy to get enthusiasm from those people who have been through it and have seen the benefits; they're easy, they're pushovers.

"All it takes is to win one, and you know what it feels like. In fifteen years with the company, as a store manager and assistant, my store has won four times.

"The little things make it, like vacuuming a flower shop canopy that's very close to the ceiling. The enthusiasm comes right from the top. Your store reflects the way you feel. Sometimes that's not fair, but that's the way it is. If the store manager puts a lot into it, then it's a reflection. It's not just once a year; you do this everyday.

"The things that motivate me are . . . I care a lot about my people. And because I care about my people, I care about my customers. I do an awful lot of counseling with my people, their personal and work problems. You work through your people. It's like that year around, and it's very easy to give that little extra effort. It works. I don't know how anybody could do otherwise."

Jasper Hughes is a part-time associate in the produce

department at Store 35. He says, "'Company's Coming' brings everybody together. This is the time when almost everybody is doing their best. Everybody's concerned about the department, more so than at other times. In our own little ways, we contribute personal items; for example, if I punched out, I might run out and get lunch for everybody so they won't have to leave and take a lunch break. There are many little things like that.

"It's a motivator that the top brass at Giant came up with that really pays off because, even if it's just once a year, it brings everybody together to a challenge. We have our buttons that say, *Only the Best.* I take that seriously, because if I have on a badge saying *Only the Best,* and you come in and I give you lousy service—well, I just couldn't do that. I think the company itself and the little things they do give us the edge.

"One time I remember more than others is when I was not scheduled to work the day before 'Company's Coming.' I had contributed quite a bit, and I planned to go down and visit my parents. In fact, I had planned that before I knew the date for 'Company's Coming.' I contributed quite a bit all during that week, so when it got down to the day before, I stopped in before I left to make sure everything was going good. Well, our department was quite a bit behind. Of course I cancelled my trip until the next day and stayed and worked . . . and Produce came in first, and the manager recognized that I made the difference. That made me feel good. I've been here since 1973. This is my store."

### TAKE THE ESSENTIALS AND APPLY THEM TO YOUR ORGANIZATION

"Company's Coming" is Giant's campaign, developed over many years, to meet their own needs. The program touches on all the levers of leadership. It makes big use of small actions; it looks for out-of-character behavior, throwing away the past and striving for new excellence; it creates an effective climate which reinforces the entire company culture; and it calls forth the commitment people have to their company. For Giant Food, nothing could be more natural.

# Endnotes

**Introduction**

[1]Ann Overton, "A Conversation With Sidney Rittenberg," *The Network Review*, 1, no. 3 (May 1983), p. 4.

[2]Maxwell Maltz, *Psycho-Cybernetics* (New York: Pocket Books, 1969), p. xiii.

**Chapter 1**

[1]John Wiebusch, ed., *Lombardi* (Chicago: Follett Publishing Co., 1971), p. 171.

**Chapter 2**

[1]John Wiebusch, ed., *Lombardi* (Chicago: Follett Publishing Co., 1971), p. 63.

[2]Maxwell Maltz, *Psycho-Cybernetics* (New York: Pocket Books, 1969), p. xiii.

[3]Wiebusch, *Lombardi,* pp. 42, 48.

**Chapter 3**

[1]John Wiebusch, ed., *Lombardi* (Chicago: Follett Publishing Co., 1971), p. 48.

[2]Ibid., p. 37.

**Chapter 4**

[1]John Wiebusch, ed., *Lombardi* (Chicago: Follett Publishing Co., 1971), p. 70.

[2]Ralph Waldo Emerson, *Nature, Addresses and Lectures* (Boston: James Munroe and Co., 1849).

[3]Craig R. Hickman and Michael A. Silva, *Creating Excellence* (New York: New American Library, 1984), see Chapter 4.

[4]Richard Tanner Pascale and Anthony G. Athos, *The Art of Japanese Management* (New York: Simon and Schuster, 1981), pp. 157–161.

## Chapter 5

[1]Richard Tanner Pascale and Anthony G. Athos, *The Art of Japanese Management* (New York: Simon and Schuster, 1981), pp. 177–192.

[2]"Hughes Circles: Eight Years and Going Strong," Rieker Management Systems *Update,* September 30, 1983, p. 4.

[3]F. Cecil Hill and William E. Courtright, "Quality Circles Work!" *IAQC Quarterly* 3rd Quarter, 1978, p. 29.

[4]Myron Magnet, "Managing by Mystique at Tandem Computers," *Fortune,* June 28, 1982, p. 86.

[5]Ibid., p. 91.

[6]"International Business Machines," *Fortune,* January 1940, pp. 36–43.

[7]John A. Young, "The Quality Focus at Hewlett-Packard," *The Journal of Business Strategy,* V, no. 3 (Winter 1985), pp. 6–9.

## Chapter 6

[1]William Ouchi, *Theory Z* (Reading, MA: Addison-Wesley Publishing Co., 1981), pp. 5–10.

[2]Jay Hall, *The Competence Process* (The Woodlands, TX: Teleometrics International, 1980), p. 28.

# Index

TO: Ken and Linda Schatz, P.O. Box 22874, Alexandria, VA 22304

FROM: (Please print) _____

ORGANIZATION: _____

ADDRESS: _____

_____

PHONE: _____

I want to know more about how Schatz and Company can help me implement *Managing By Influence* in my organization.

I'm particularly interested in:

☐ A speech for _____ people.

☐ In-house seminars for _____ people.

☐ Attending a public seminar.

☐ A speech for a professional/trade association meeting, or a convention.

Other comments: _____

_____

_____

_____

_____

Signed _____

Date _____